Basel Committee on Banking Supervision

Basel Committee on Banking Supervision

A Primer on Governance, History, and Legitimacy—Part 1

By

Maziar Peihani

BRILL

LEIDEN | BOSTON

Library of Congress Control Number: 2016942915

Typeface for the Latin, Greek, and Cyrillic scripts: “Brill”. See and download: brill.com/brill-typeface.

ISBN 978-90-04-32812-9 (paperback)
ISBN 978-90-04-32844-0 (e-book)

Originally published as Volume 1(1) 2016, in *International Banking and Securities Law*,
DOI 10.1163/24056936-12340001.

This book is printed on acid-free paper and produced in a sustainable manner.

Contents

Basel Committee on Banking Supervision

A Primer on Governance, History, and Legitimacy—Part 1

Maziar Peihani
Postdoctoral Fellow, Centre for Banking and Finance Law,
National University of Singapore

Abstract

The Basel Committee on Banking Supervision (BCBS) was established in 1974 as an informal group of central bankers and bank supervisors with the mandate to formulate supervisory standards and guidelines. Although the Committee does not have any formal supranational authority, it is the de facto global banking regulator and its recommendations have been widely implemented by member and non-member states. This project investigates the BCBS's governance, operation, and policy outcomes to determine the extent to which it is and has been legitimate. The project is comprised of two parts. This part overviews the literature on the BCBS, outlines its contribution, and provides a primer on the Committee's governance and functions. In addition, it engages with the current theories on legitimacy and discusses what legitimacy means for the global governance of banking and how it can be assessed.

Keywords

accountability – banking regulation – Basel Committee – Global Financial Crisis – legitimacy

Section 1. Introduction

Introduction

The global financial crisis (GFC) of 2008 was the most destructive economic event since the Great Depression. Many of us who lived through the crisis will easily remember the shocking events that took place: stock prices went down dramatically; investors lost their confidence in the market and pulled their money out; large and famous financial institutions failed or teetered on the brink of bankruptcy; the global credit markets ceased to function and liquidity vanished from the system; governments were scrambling to prevent the

 | DOI 10.1163/9789004328440_002

collapse of the whole system with massive taxpayer-funded bailouts.[1] According to the US Treasury, the crisis cost US households $19.2 trillion in wealth and 8.8 million jobs.[2] During the crisis, member states of the European Union (EU) committed to aid banks in the amount of approximately 30% of the EU GDP and paid out amounts equivalent to 13% of EU GDP.[3] The economic costs of the GFC in terms of output losses and increases in public debt was much larger than all crises occurring in the previous thirty years in advanced and emerging economies combined. The median output loss (computed as deviations of actual output from its trend) during the GFC (from 2007 to 2009) was 25% of GDP compared to a historical median of 20%, while the median increase in public debt is 24% of GDP compared to a historical median of 16%.[4]

---

1 The turmoil originated with the credit contraction in the interbank markets beginning 9 August 2007. The interbank credit froze after BNP Paribas suspended payments on three investment funds. The German Sachsen Landesbank was sold to the Landesbank Baden-Wuerttenberg on 28 August 2007 and IKB lost $1 billion in subprime loans. Shares in Northern Rock, a British bank that had invested heavily in sub-prime mortgages, fell on 14 and 15 September 2007, following the announcement of its request for liquidity support from the Bank of England. In United States, the collapse of the housing bubble and the abrupt shutdown of subprime lending had led to substantial losses for many financial institutions. On 17 March 2008, the Federal Reserve, using its authority under s. 13(3) of the Federal Reserve Act, announced $29.97 billion to enable JP Morgan to purchase Bear Sterns for $2 per share. The crisis then reached a critical stage in September 2008 with the failure of Lehman Brothers and the near collapse of the American International Group (AIG). The lack of transparency of the balance sheets of the major financial institutions, which were "too big to fail", and had a high level of interconnections, caused the credit market to seize up. In the five days between Monday, 15 September and Friday, 19 September, the global financial system was teetering on collapse. Even after the US government announced a $700 billion bailout plan, namely the Troubled Asset Relief Program (TARP), the US markets slightly stabilized. In Europe the EU leaders could not agree on a collective response. This failure then forced the British government to take the lead in announcing a comprehensive rescue package totaling £ 500 billion of loans and guaranties. See George A Walker, "Credit contraction, Financial Collapse and Global Recession: pt 1", (2009) 1 JIBFL 5; A Cohen, "Global Financial Crisis—Timeline" (2009) 1 JIBFL 10.

2 US Department of Treasury, "The Financial Crisis Response In Charts" (2012) at 1, online: US Treasury. http://www.treasury.gov/resource-center/data-chart-center/Documents/20120413_FinancialCrisisResponse.pdf.

3 Herman V. Rompuy, "Reshaping Europe's Economy—The Role of the Financial Sector" (2011) at 3, online: EU http://www.consilium.europa.eu/uedocs/cms_data/docs/pressdata/en/ec/119231.pdf.

4 Luc Laeven & Fabian Valencia, "Resolution of Banking Crises: The Good, the Bad, and the Ugly" (IMF Working Paper, WP/10/146, June 2010) at 4.

There has been enormous debate about the causes of the GFC.[5] However, one common narrative is that the crisis was an *incident* that took everyone, particularly regulators, by surprise.[6] Under this narrative, the years preceding the crisis witnessed a major saving glut, which led to large flows of capital into several major economies. These flows in turn triggered lower interest rates, investors' turn to high-yield risky structured products, and explosion of credit.[7] Together, these factors brought about a crisis that Alan Greenspan has likened to a "hundred-year flood" unforeseen by all.[8] Inadequate legal authority, an incomplete toolkit to combat the financial market's fragility, and insurmountable regulatory gaps are among the themes commonly referred to by those who subscribe to the view that the GFC was a complex and severe crisis.[9]

---

5 See, e.g., Howard Davis, *The Financial Crisis: Who is to Blame* (Cambridge: Polity Press, 2010); Marc Jarsulic, *Anatomy of a Financial Crisis: A Real Estate Bubble, Runaway Credit Markets, and Regulatory Failure* (New York: Palgrave, 2010); Robert Kolb, ed., *Lessons from the Financial Crisis: Causes, Consequences, and Our Economic Future* (New Jersey: Wiley, 2010); Joseph Stiglitz et al., *The Stiglitz Report: Reforming the International Monetary and Financial Systems In the Wake of the Global Crisis* (New York: The New Press, 2010); John B. Taylor, *Getting Off Track: How Government Actions and Interventions Caused, Prolonged, and Worsened the Financial Crisis* (California: Hoover Institution Press, 2009); Mathias Dewatripont et al., *Balancing the Banks: Global Lessons from the Financial Crisis* (Princeton: Princeton University Press, 2010); Hershey H. Friedman & Linda W. Friedman, "The Global Financial Crisis of 2008: What Went Wrong?" (March 9, 2009) online: Social Sciences and research Network: http://dx.doi.org/10.2139/ssrn.1356193; Sher Verick & Iyanatul Islam, "The Great Recession of 2008–2009: Causes, Consequences and Policy Responses", IZA Discussion Paper No. 4934 (2009) online: Social Sciences and research Network http://papers.ssrn.com/sol3/papers.cfm?abstract_id=1631069; Douglas W Arner, "The Global Credit Crisis of 2008: Causes and Consequences", AIIFL Working Paper No. 3 (2009) online: Social Sciences and research Network http://papers.ssrn.com/sol3/papers.cfm?abstract_id=1330744.

6 See, James R. Barth, Gerard Caprio Jr. & Ross Levine, *Guardians of Finance: Making Regulators Work for Us* (Cambridge, MA: MIT Press, 2012) at 1–4. The authors provide an eloquent explanation of the incident narrative.

7 Timothy F. Geithner, "Reducing Systemic Risk in a Dynamic Financial System" (Remarks at the Economic Club of New York, New York City, 9 June 2008) online: Federal Reserve Bank of New York http://www.newyorkfed.org/newsevents/speeches/2008/tfg080609.html.

8 Alan Greenspan, "The Crisis" in David Homer & Justin Wolfers, eds, *Brookings Papers on Economic Activity* (Brookings Instituion Press, 2010) 201 at 216.

9 On inadequate legal authority, see, e.g., Christopher Cox, Address (Speech delivered at the Security Traders 12th Annual Washington Conference, 7 May 2008) online: US Securities and Exchange Commission http://www.sec.gov/news/speech/2008/spch050708cc.htm; On incomplete toolkit to manage financial crises, see Timothy F. Geithner, (Written Testimony House Financial Services Committee Hearing, 24 march 2009), online: US Department of Treasury http://www.treasury.gov/press-center/press-releases/Pages/tg67.aspx;

As Timothy Geithner said after the AIG bailout, "If we could have done it differently, we would have done it differently. Instead, we had no other choice. That is the basic lesson of this great recession."[10]

There is some merit to the incident narrative. When the Crisis exploded, panics, runs, and massive failures appeared inevitable and policy makers needed to take immediate action to thwart financial contagion and assuage the impact of the Crisis. However, the incident narrative, is at the same time, a woefully incomplete account of the crisis. The housing boom, the surge of subprime mortgages, the massive leverage, and the proliferation of complex structured products were trends closely watched by regulators and policy makers.[11]

On regulatory gaps, see Timothy F. Geithner, Address (Remarks Remarks before the American Enterprise Institute on Financial Reform, 22 March 2010) online: US Department of Treasury http://www.treasury.gov/press-center/press-releases/Pages/tg600.aspx; Christopher Cox, "The State of the United States Economy and Financial Markets" (Testimony Before the U.S. Senate Committee on Banking, Housing and Urban Affairs, 14 February 2008) online: US Securities and Exchange Commission http://www.sec.gov/news/testimony/2008/ts021408cc.htm.

10 Timothy F. Geithner, Address (Secretary Written Testimony before the House Committee on Oversight and Government Reform, 27 January 2010) online: US Department of Treasury http://www.treasury.gov/press-center/press-releases/Pages/tg514.aspx.

11 From 1997 until the middle of 2006, house prices began to rise much more rapidly than building costs or general price levels in the US. While nominal house prices increased at annual rate of 9.3%, building costs only increased at an annual rate of 2.9% and consumer price index at an annual rate of 2.5%. Between 1953 and 1997 (a period of 45 years) housing prices remained basically unchanged. It was, therefore, a historical anomaly when housing prices increased 85% between 1997 and 2006. The Federal Reserve had knowledge of this irregularity and continued appreciation of housing prices. However, Alan Greenspan, its former Chairman, told audiences "that we were facing not a bubble but froth—lots of small local bubbles that never grew to a scale that could threaten the health of the overall economy." See, Alan Greenspan, *The Age of Turbulence: Adventures in a New World* (New York: Penguin Press, 2007) at 231; Jarsulic, *supra* note 5 at 12–13; Karl E. Case & Robert Shiller, "Is There a Bubble in the Housing Market?" (Brookings Paper on. Economic Activity, No. 2, 2003): Brookings Institution http://www.brookings.edu/~/media/Files/Programs/ES/BPEA/2003_2_bpea_papers/2003b_bpea_caseshiller.pdf.

From 2001 through 2003, the value of subprime loans almost doubled to $310 billion. The volume of subprime mortgages then increased from 8% of mortgage originations in 2003 to 20% in 2005. Regulators were aware of the dangers of the subprime market but chose not to curb its expansion. Greenspan considered it undesirable to rein in subprime lending. In his view, subprime products and practices were not necessarily improper. On the contrary, they could facilitate "the national policy of making homeownership more broadly available". His successor, Ben Bernanke, also believed that the impact of the subprime market turmoil on the financial markets and the broader

It is even more troubling to consider that the Crisis occurred despite the existence of a comprehensive body of international financial standards (IFS) that had been developed over the previous 35 years.[12] At the time of Crisis, the IFS covered 12 areas of financial activity including banking, securities, corporate

---

economy "seem[ed] likely to be contained". The Office of Federal Housing Enterprise Oversight (OFHEO), which was in charge of overseeing the operations of Fannie Mae and Freddie Mac, knew about the purchase of subprime mortgages-backed securities by these firms. In its 2004 examination, however, it mentioned that such mortgages were not a "significant supervisory concern" and satisfactory credit risk management was in place. See, The Financial Crisis Inquiry Commission, "Final Report of the National Commission on the Causes of the Financial and economic Crisis in the United States" (January 2011) at 93–94, 123, online: FCIC http://cybercemetery.unt.edu/archive/FCIC/20110310173545/http://c0182732.cdn1.cloudfiles.rackspacecloud.com/FCIC_final_report_full.pdf; Ben Bernanke, "The Economic Outlook" (Testimony before the Joint Economic Committee, U.S. Congress, 28 March 2007) online: http://www.federalreserve.gov/newsevents/testimony/bernanke20070328a.htm.

From 2002 to 2007 financial markets observed a staggering growth in securitization. In the aggregate, securitization worldwide went from $767 billion at the end of 2001 to $1.4 trillion in 2004 and $2.7 trillion in December of 2006. Regulators, however, did not seem concerned with this development. The common belief was still that securitization transactions could help distribute the risk and make financial markets safer. In a speech delivered in June 2006, Ben Bernanke said:

"To an important degree, banks can be more active in their management of credit risks and other portfolio risks because of the increased availability of financial instruments and activities such as loan syndications, loan trading, credit derivatives, and securitization ... Asset-backed securitization has also provided a vehicle for decreasing concentrations and credit risk in bank portfolios by permitting the sale of loans in the capital markets, particularly loans on homes and commercial real estate."

Similarly, the IMF's Global Financial Stability Report of April, 2006 stated: "The dispersion of credit risk by banks to a broader and more diverse set of investors, rather than warehousing such risk on their balance sheets, has helped make the banking and overall financial system more resilient". It noted that this dispersion would help to "mitigate and absorb shocks to the financial system". See, Viral V. Acharya & Matthew Richardson, "Causes of the Financial Crisis" (2009) at 7–8, online: SSRN http://ssrn.com/abstract=1514984; Arnold Kling, "Not What They Had in Mind: A History of Policies that Produced the Financial Crisis of 2008" (15 September 2009) at 27–28, online: SSRN http://ssrn.com/abstract=3D1474430; Ben Bernanke, "Modern Risk Management and Banking Supervision" (12 June 2006), online: Federal Reserve http://www.federalreserve.gov/newsevents/speech/Bernanke20060612a.htm; IMF, "Global Financial Stability Report—April 2006", at 51, online: IMF.http://www.imf.org/External/Pubs/FT/GFSR/2006/01/pdf/chp2.pdf.

12 FSB, "Compendium of Standards" (Accessed on 25 April 2016) http://www.financialstabilityboard.org/cos/index.htm.

governance, and accounting.[13] In spite of their scope and sophistication, not only did the IFS not prevent the Crisis but also contributed to it in significant ways. The failure of the IFS is most evident in the context of international capital adequacy standards, commonly known as the Basel Accords.[14] Basel Accords encompass prudential standards. These standards depart from the premise that banks occupy a special position in the financial system given banks' central role in the payment and credit network and their vulnerability to loss of confidence.[15] A bank run is not only a threat to the bank itself but can pose risks to the entire financial system and broader economy. To rule out externalities arising from bank runs, authorities establish safety net mechanisms such as deposit insurance and lender of last resort.[16] These mechanisms, however, impose costs on taxpayers and, more importantly, could exacerbate moral hazard by encouraging banks to take excessive risk.[17] To address these problems regulators go beyond disclosure requirements and market discipline and subject banks to prudential regulation.[18]

However, Basel Accords failed to achieve their intended objectives, namely ensuring the stability and soundness of the banking system. The Accords proved to be inadequate, pro-cyclical, and excessively reliant on internal risk modeling and credit ratings. There were also no minimum standards that could protect the system against the liquidity risk. The failure of Basel Accords raises important questions about the body out of which they are conceived, namely the Basel Committee on banking Supervision (BCBS), which is the principal agent investigated in this research. Similar to many other international regimes, the BCBS is a problem-driven institution. The primary purpose for its establishment was to tackle risks arising from the operations of internationally active banks. The Committee's authority is therefore often justified based on the utilities delivered, namely a safer and sounder international banking system. However, such perception of *output legitimacy* is challenged by the failure

13 FSB, "Key Standards for Sound Financial Systems" (Accessed on 25 April 2016) online: FSB http://www.financialstabilityboard.org/cos/key_standards.htm.

14 BCBS, "The Basel Committee's Work" (Accessed on 25 April 2016) online: BIS http://www.bis.org/bcbs/bcbs_work.htm.

15 Charles E. Goodhart et al., *Financial Regulation: Why, How and Where Now* (London: Routledge, 1998) at 10–12; Peter Brierley, "The UK Special Resolution Regime for Failing Banks in an International Context" (2009) at 5, online: Bank of England http://www.bankofengland.co.uk/publications/fsr/fs_paper05.pdf.

16 Howard Davies & David Green, *Global Financial Regulation—The Essential Guide* (Cambridge: Polity, 2008) at 16–17.

17 *Ibid.*, at 18.

18 *Ibid.*, at 19–20.

of the most important policy outcome of the BCBS, namely, capital adequacy standards.

Although the GFC has been associated with systemic regulatory failures, the question of how to make regulators more accountable has been largely overlooked. A glance at recent initiatives in the areas of prudential regulation, corporate governance, derivatives and consumer protection indicates that the post-crisis reform agenda mainly seeks to promote responsible behaviour by market participants. Undoubtedly, the Crisis revealed significant market failures. In order to address these failures, regulators should incentivize market participants to act more responsibly and avoid the type of risk taking that can lead to externalities for all of society. However, when it is acknowledged that the role of regulatory failures in the Crisis was as important—if not more so—than that of market failures, the issue of regulator accountability gains equal significance.

Inadequate research of regulatory governance and accountability is apparent with respect to international institutions, particularly the BCBS, which has been central to the global governance regime of banking. The Committee is the oldest and best-known global regulatory forum, and the primary global prudential standard setter. The Committee's standards, guidelines and sound practices have been widely implemented and countries look to the Committee's leadership with respect to regulatory and supervisory issues. However, as the following literature review will demonstrate, the BCBS's governance and policy making has been subject to little research—a research gap that motivated this project. As this section explains, my primary project is that there are considerable steps that the BCBS must take in order to become a more accountable global standard setter.

Overview of the Literature on the BCBS

To date, the BCBS has been subject to three comprehensive studies. The first study was "The Basel Committee on Banking Supervision: A History of the Early Years, 1974–1997" by Charles Goodhart. An important feature of this book is that the author was the first to be given access to the BCBS's papers and archives, including the records of the 83 meetings that occurred in the period covered by the book.[19]

The book provides an in-depth and comprehensive narrative of the BCBS's history. Goodhart's main aim is to tell the story of the BCBS's evolution as the Committee itself saw it. In other words, the book chiefly seeks to produce a quasi-official public record of the BCBS, with a lot of "cut and paste" of original

---

19 Charles A. E. Goodhart, *The Basel Committee on Banking Supervision: A History of the Early Years, 1974–1997* (Cambridge, UK; New York: Cambridge University Press, 2011) at xi–xii.

documents which can be useful for future historians.[20] The bulk of the book is about the BCBS's work in the covered period, including Concordat, the First Capital Accord, and the Core Principles of Banking Supervision. It also provides short commentaries on issues such as the BCBS's legal position, and its international relations with its counterparts.[21]

Professor Goodhart's book is a significant contribution to the literature on the history of financial regulation in general and the BCBS in particular. My project particularly benefited from the book's research on how and why the BCBS was created and its evolution during its first two decades. However, it needs to kept in mind that the book's history ends with 1997, a year when the BCBS started to think about new stages of capital adequacy regulation. Consequently, the Basel II exercise, which became the focus of the BCBS in subsequent years, is excluded from the book. The reason that Goodhart offers for such exclusion is that the Basel II initiative is "too recent and for the time being too contentious to become subject of a historical study such as this."[22] Be that as it may, the book also does not provide an account of the current status of the BCBS and major changes it has undergone in more recent years.

The second important study is "International Banking Regulation: Law, Policy, and Practice" by George Walker.[23] The book's purpose is to consider the structure and content of regulation that apply to banks at the international level. Similar to Goodhart's book, this manuscript begins by explaining the circumstances surrounding the establishment the Basel Committee following the collapse of the Bretton Woods System of managed exchanged rates and the subsequent closures of Franklin National and Banhus Herstatt.[24] The book then turns to explain the structure and operation of the BCBS and assesses its contribution to international bank regulation and supervision. In addition to drawing upon publicly available sources of information, the book benefits from personal interviews with Central bankers and supervisors who were closely involved in the BCBS's agenda setting and policy making in its early years, such as Peter Cooke, the former BCBS Chairman.[25]

The book pays particular attention to cross-sector and cross-border regulatory issues that arise from the increasingly integrated activities of complex

---

20 *Ibid.*, at xii.

21 *Ibid.*, at 96–371, 542–571.

22 *Ibid.*, at 7.

23 George A. Walker, *International Banking Regulation: Law, Policy, and Practice* (London, UK, Kluwer, 2001).

24 *Ibid.*, at 17–34.

25 *Ibid.*, at xix.

banking and financial groups.[26] Walker considers the background context for the rise of financial conglomerates and provides a detailed assessment of the international response to their risks.[27] Another important contribution of the book is its careful consideration of the nature and content of capital adequacy standards at the time.

While the book was written at a point when the Committee's work on Basel II was at a very early stage, the book considers the BCBS's preliminary proposals and their impact on the banking regulatory regime.[28]

From the perspective of this project, an important contribution of this book is the explanation of the nature of modern regulatory requirements and the relationship between law and regulation. Walker notes that banking regulation does not fit with any of the traditional definitions or classifications of national or international law to the extent that it is not imposed in the form of primary or secondary legislation and is not backed by any formal court processes.[29] He acknowledges, however, that many, if not all, of the obligations imposed on banks operate within a large legal framework. Compliance with regulatory requirements is not secured through court adjudication and formal enforcement but through a range of formal and informal devices and controls. Thus, bank regulations have the equivalent significance of a legal obligation without falling within category of law as such.[30]

The third important study on the BCBS is "Governing Global Banking: the Basel Committee and the Politics of Financial Globalization". Adopting a largely historical approach, Duncan Wood traces the evolution of the Basel Committee from its origin in the 1970s to its early years in the 21st century. The author's hypoproject is that the evolution of the BCBS has been driven by the need for banking authorities in the major economies to respond to challenges in the changing market place. In other words, it was the serious risks posed by profit-seeking practices of financial institutions that necessitated increasing cooperation among the banking supervisors from the world's major financial institutions.

Wood argues that the BCBS has continued to respond effectively to new problems and crises in the post-Bretton Woods era. Although the Committee has not eliminated crises from national or international banking systems, its existence and work has greatly contributed to the stability and soundness of

26 *Ibid.*, Part II Financial Conglomerates.

27 *Ibid.*

28 *Ibid.*, Part V Postscript.

29 *Ibid.*, at xxii.

30 *Ibid.*

the international financial system. According to Wood, the BCBS's limited success can be explained by reference to three factors: the will of powerful states to create an agenda for cooperation; the influence of private actors in national policy processes; and the capacity of the Committee to avoid or overcome conflict between its members.[31] Power, leadership, the influence of private sectors, and the dynamic relationship between regulators and markets are among the key themes of the book. The book's contribution is thus best understood from a political economy perspective. Wood's inquiry builds upon earlier contributions of political economists such as Ethan Kapstein, Tony Porter and Beth Simmons who have highlighted the importance of elements of power and coercion in the area of international banking cooperation.[32]

The most important insight that this project takes away from Wood's analysis is that politics is essential and central to an adequate understanding of the BCBS. Though the Committee has been frequently idealized as purely technical—an epistemic community of specialists engaging in technocratic deliberations—Wood's novel contribution indicates that politics has marked every step of the BCBS's work and evolution.[33] The centrality of politics is conspicuous in the Basel II process, which was characterized by the emergence of ideological divisions between the Anglo-Saxon states on the one hand and the Continental European states on the other hand.[34] The book also provides important empirical evidence regarding the influence of the banking sector in the notice and comment process, which this project discusses in addressing the narrative of regulatory capture.

Contribution of Project

The existing books on the BCBS make important contributions to the understanding of BCBS's history, governance, and policies. However, they are written in reference to a state of affairs that appears quite out of date. There can

---

31 Duncan Wood, *Governing Global Banking: the Basel Committee and the Politics of Financial Globalization* (Aldershot, Hants, England; Ashgate, 2005) at 4–5.

32 See for instance, Ethan B. Kapstein, Resolving the Regulator's Dilemma: International Coordination of Banking Regulations", (2009) 53:2 *International Organization* 323; Ethan B. Kapstein, Supervising International Banks: Origins and Implications of the Basle Accord (Princeton, NJ: Princeton university, 1991); Ethan B. Kapstein, *Governing the Global Economy: International Finance and the State* (Cambridge, MA: Harvard University, 1994); Tony Porter, *States, Markets and Regimes In Global Finance* (New York: St. Martin's Press, 1993); Beth A. Simmons, "The International Politics of Harmonization: the Case of Capital Markets Regulation", (2001) 55:3 *International Organization* 589.

33 Wood, *supra* note 31 at 163–164.

34 *Ibid.*, at 123–148.

be little doubt, if any, that the recent Crisis has transformed the governance and regulation of international banking. For instance, the BCBS is no longer a standing Committee of G10 but a reporting Committee to G20, which has in recent years become the primary forum for global economic cooperation.[35] The Committee's membership has been expanded twice to include emerging markets and developing economies.[36] The basis for the BCBS's operations is no longer an informal press statement,[37] but a new *Charter* which sets out its structure, mandate and function in some detail.[38] The BCBS's operations have been subjected to oversight of a higher body, designated as the Group of Governors and Heads of Supervision.[39] Last but not the least, the Committee has adopted any array of new policies in response to the recent crisis. Basel III is the most important of such policies, the implementation of which is now monitored by the BCBS.[40]

The current literature on the BCBS does not engage with these new developments. Nor do they engage with questions of legitimacy and accountability, which warrant immediate attention in the face of massive regulatory failures. My research seeks to make a positive contribution towards filling these gaps. It investigates the BCBS's governance, operation, and policy outcomes to determine the extent to which it is and has been legitimate. The point of departure for my analysis is the literature on legitimacy in law, political science, and international relations. In particular, I draw upon Global Administrative Law (GAL) theory to examine the BCBS's legitimacy against three principles of reasoned decision making, transparency, and accountability. I argue that the BCBS has gradually become a more legitimate institution but that significant room still exists for improvement. Inadequate disclosure on the BCBS's deliberations, underrepresentation of constituencies without business interest or insufficient financial resources in BCBS consultations, and absence of

35 See, e.g., G20, "Monitoring Adoption of Basel III Standards and Reports to the G20" (Accessed on 25 April 2016) online: BIS http://www.bis.org/bcbs/implementation/bprl1.htm.

36 BCBS. "Basel Committee broadens its membership" (2009) online: BIS http://www.bis.org/press/p090610.htm; BCBS, "Expansion of Membership Announced by the Basel Committee" (2009) online: BIS http://www.bis.org/press/p090313.htm.

37 See, "Note on the BIS Governors' Activities vis-à-vis the Euro-currency Market" (12 February 1975), reprinted in Goodhart, *supra* note 19 at 50.

38 BCBS, "Basel Committee on Banking Supervision (BCBS) Charter" (January 2013) online: BIS http://www.bis.org/bcbs/charter.htm [*Charter*].

39 *Charter, ibid.*, s 6.

40 BCBS, "International Regulatory Framework for Banks (Basel III)" (Accessed on 25 April 2016) online: BIS http://www.bis.org/bcbs/basel3.htm.

meaningful oversight of the BCBS's policies, are among the areas that I highlight for reform. I set out policy prescriptions to enhance the BCBS's legitimacy, including the establishment of a new framework for transparency; creation of a proxy advocate to participate on behalf of underrepresented constituencies in the BCBS's policy making; and the establishment of a new body, which I designate as the Independent Evaluation Committee, to exercise active oversight of the BCBS's operations.

Overview of Project

The inquiry begins by taking a closer look at what legitimacy means and how it can be assessed for the global governance of banking. A taxonomy of legitimacy is developed, drawing upon four established bases for the acceptance of a governing authority: 1) majority will and representation, 2) dialogue and deliberation, 3) stability and coherence of rules, and 4) expertise and competence to generate material benefits. The discussion illustrates the contested nature of legitimacy and the insights that can be drawn from different theories for assessing legitimacy at the supranational level. I argue that while institutions of global governance often lack direct mechanisms of democracy, such as elections, nurturing other accepted bases for legitimacy can further legitimize them. In particular, I will draw upon GAL to argue that the BCBS can become more legitimate by meeting adequate standards of reasoned decision making, transparency, consultation, and oversight.

Section 3 explores the BCBS's history and current position in the global regulatory sphere. It aims to establish a general understanding of the BCBS's evolution and current governance and serve as a background for the analyses in subsequent sections. The section traces the origins of the BCBS to the drastic changes that took place in the system of international banking in 1960s and 1970s and illustrates how the BCBS grew from a forum merely for informal education and exchange of information on banking supervision to a primary global standard setter for prudential regulation of banks. Particular attention is paid to the post-crisis governance and operation of the BCBS and its current position in the International financial architecture. The section posits that the BCBS can be best understood as a transnational regulatory network that has dispensed with traditional formalities associated with formal international organizations. The networked governance of the BCBS represents both opportunities and challenges with respect to its legitimacy. For instance, strong peer-to-peer ties among bank supervisors, twinned with institutional flexibility and consensus-based decision making can be viewed as enhancing the deliberative quality of the BCBS's policy making. On the other hand, closed operation of the BCBS and its exclusive membership of officials from central banks and supervisory authorities, who have similar education and career backgrounds, expose the Committee to groupthink problems and the risk of adopting inferior policies.

Section 4 assesses the BCBS's legitimacy and accountability based on the criteria identified in the theoretical framework (Section 2). Four crucial questions drive this section's assessment: 1) Does the BCBS give reasons for its decisions? 2) Are the Committee's governance and decision-making procedures transparent? 3) How and by what means does the BCBS consult the public in its policy-making process? 4) How and by who is the Committee's performance monitored? Since the BCBS has produced a massive body of standards over the years, my assessment of reasoned decision making focuses on the Basel III process which has produced one of the most important post-crisis regulatory reforms. The analysis of the BCBS's transparency is conducted around three focal points: internal governance, decision-making procedures, and implementation of standards. In regard to consultation, I consider both the sources of input for the BCBS's policy making and the notice and comment process, which is used to consult the public on the BCBS's major policy proposals. In addition to examining the origin of the notice and comment, I investigate its operation in the Basel II and Basel III processes. I am particularly concerned with the question of 'who' participates in the process and engage with the political economy literature on regulatory capture as it applies to the BCBS's interaction with private interests. Finally, Section 4 assesses the oversight arrangements for the BCBS's policy making at the international level. In particular, it focuses on two supranational bodies that currently exercise oversight over the BCBS: the Group of Governors and Heads of Supervision (GHOS) and the G20. The GHOS has been expressly designated as the BCBS oversight body in the *Charter* and appears to have been in operation since 2009.[41] The G20 does not have any formal authority over the BCBS but it seems noteworthy for the purpose of this analysis given the influence that it exercises over the post-crisis financial reform.

The findings of my assessment indicate that the BCBS does not score equally on all criteria. The best score seems to be achieved on reasoned decision making given the sound administrative procedures that the BCBS followed during the Basel III process, such as public invitation for comments, clear articulation of reforms' objectives, and timely costs and benefits analyses. Considerable progress can be also observed on the transparency front. The adoption of the notice and comment, the online disclosure of policy documents and the newly-adopted *Charter* has made the Committee's work more visible to the public.

41 *Charter, supra* note 38, s 6.

Important information gaps, however, remain regarding the BCBS's internal governance and decision making, especially the BCBS's deliberations which are subject to little and selective disclosure.

The assessment of the BCBS's consultation indicates greater legitimacy gaps and room for improvement based on the previous two criteria (reasoned decision making and transparency). The real benefits of notice and comment cannot be overstated given that it has been mostly used as a lobbying tool by banks rather than as a mechanism for conveying the demands and concerns of a broad set of stakeholders. Moreover, notice and comment cannot always facilitate timely input given that it is only used for completed draft proposals. The lowest score seems to be achieved on oversight, given that neither GHOS nor G20 exercise meaningful oversight over the BCBS. The technical nature of the BCBS's work and lack of independence on the part of oversight bodies are among the factors that can explain this weak oversight.

Section 5 contains the concluding remarks. It posits that legitimacy appears to be a matter of degree. An institution is not simply legitimate or illegitimate but rather more legitimate or less legitimate, depending on how it scores on legitimacy criteria. Institutional change and direction must also be considered when evaluating legitimacy; an institution whose legitimacy is deteriorating is more questionable than that of an institution that is improving. Applying the above criteria to the issue at hand, the BCBS has indeed become incrementally more legitimate since its inception. It discloses more information on its operations and policies and attempts to engage with the public through notice and comment. Its performance and policies are subject to some form of oversight by a superior body. The committee has also been responsive to public concerns about drawbacks of prudential standards and has taken important corrective measures. Nevertheless, as this project's assessments show, there is considerable room for the BCBS to become more legitimate. Thus Section 6 outlines some recommendations for improved BCBS legitimacy. These recommendations have been grouped around five major categories: enhancing reasoned decision making and transparency; creating new consultation mechanisms; enhancing the BCBS accountability at the national and international level; and making the BCBS a more inclusive global standard setter. The policy recommendations are subject to two important caveats. First, they are by nature preliminary, as they represent the first attempt in the literature to make the BCBS more legitimate. Second, the institutional supply of such reforms as enhanced transparency and consultation must be met by strong societal demand for public interest banking regulation to emerge.

It needs to be noted that this manuscript is published in two parts. As a result, the first part only includes Sections 1 to 3 and the remainder of the manuscript, namely Sections 4 and 5, will be published subsequently in the second part. The original manuscript contained an extensive analysis of the BCBS policy outcomes, particularly Basel III. The author, however, decided to leave out this analysis, given the significant changes that the Basel Committee is introducing to the Basel Accords.[42] These reforms mainly concern the denominator of the regulatory capital, namely how banks calculate the risk weights of their exposures. Since the proposals are at an early stage and will be subject to substantial consultation with banks, the direction of the Committee's work and the substance of the final revisions are yet to be seen. Until then a substantive analysis of the Basel Accords and its subsequent revisions, which are so significant that some refer to it as Basel IV,[43] will be better deferred.

Section 2. An Exploration of Legitimacy: What Does It Mean for the Global Governance of Banking and How Can It Be Assessed?

Legitimacy: An Elusive Concept

The term "legitimacy" can be traced back to the Latin word *legitmus*, which was used in Roman and medieval jurisprudence to characterize a state of affairs that was in accordance with law, justice and customs.[44] Beginning in the middle ages, the concept came to represent legal succession to a throne according to the principle of primogeniture. Legitimacy then became a key political term in post-colonial Europe when the sovereignty of rulers (legitimacy as primogeniture) and the sovereignty of people (legitimacy as self-determination) became two competing concepts.[45]

At its most basic, the idea of legitimacy refers to rightfulness and acceptability of political authority. However, what makes political authority acceptable

42 BCBS, "Reducing Variation in Credit Risk-Weighted Assets—Constraints on the use of Internal Model Approaches—Consultative Document" (March 2016) online: BIS https://www.bis.org/bcbs/publ/d362.htm; BCBS, "Regulatory Consistency Assessment Programme (RCAP)—Analysis of Risk-Weighted Assets for Credit Risk in the Banking Book" (April 2016) online: BIS https://www.bis.org/bcbs/publ/d363.htm; BCBS, "Revisions to the Basel III Leverage Ratio Framework—Consultative Document" (April 2016) online: BIS. https://www.bis.org/bcbs/publ/d365.htm.

43 Laura Noonan, "Basel IV Spectre Looms For Battle-Worn Bankers" (14 March 2016) *The Financial Times*.

44 Achim Hurrelmann, Steffen Schneider & Jens Steffek, "Introduction: Legitimacy in an Age of Global Politics" in Achim Hurrelmann, Steffen Schneider & Jens Steffek, ed, *Legitimacy in an age of global politics* (New York: Palgrave Macmillan, 2007) at 3–4.

45 *Ibid.*

and what criteria should be used to measure legitimacy are contested questions; many commentators have used the democratic theory to answer it.[46] However, as will be illustrated below, the conception or model of democracy used in an analysis could result in different outcomes. The question also becomes more challenging when the locus of analysis is global governance institutions that, in nature and operation, are not confined to any nation state. It must also be noted that democracy is not the only premise for such an analysis; the order or stability and the performance of an institution are among other important bases of legitimacy. In the following paragraphs, I trace through four established foundations of governing authority: 1) majority will and representation; 2) dialogue and deliberation; 3) stability and coherence of rules; and 4) expertise and competence to generate material benefits. In addition to discussing their salient features, I will briefly comment on the application of these principles to global governance, as well as broader insights that can be drawn from their application. My central argument is that while institutions of global governance often lack direct mechanisms of democracy, such as elections, nurturing other accepted bases for legitimacy can further legitimize them. In particular, I will draw upon Global Administrative Law theory to argue that the BCBS can become more legitimate by meeting adequate standards of reasoned decision making, transparency, consultation, and oversight.

As an initial step, it is important to note that legitimacy can be seen from two perspectives: normative and empirical. In the former, a researcher defines and defends a set of criteria for legitimacy and then applies them to institutions or orders. This approach assesses particular regimes and produces statements of a *normative* or *diagnostic* nature. In the second case, by contrast, the researcher is particularly concerned with the conception of legitimacy held by real world actors. For instance, the researcher examines how citizens or certain elites see and evaluate legitimacy of existing institutions. This approach results in statements with an important *empirical* dimension given that the identified criteria are described as being used more or less widely and certain institutions as being more or less accepted.[47] It is important to note that even in such situation the real world actor's perception of legitimacy can be indeed normative. However, since the social scientist makes assertions based on

46 See, e.g., Fritz W. Scharpf, *Governing In Europe: Effective and Democratic?* (Oxford: Oxford University Press, 1999); David Held, *Democracy and the Global Order: Form the Modern States to Cosmopolitan Governance* (Polity Press: Cambridge, 1995); Jan A Scholte: Towards Greater Legitimacy in Global Governance (2011) 18:1 *Review of International Political Economy* 110 [Scholte, "Towards Greater Legitimacy"].

47 Hurrelmann, Schneider & Steffek, *supra* note 44 at 3–4.

cumulative evidence, his or her statements have empirical significance. What follows next is primarily concerned with a normative perspective of legitimacy. That is, it examines what different theorists identify as an appropriate basis for legitimacy, and what criteria they define and defend for their normative evaluations. However, one must be cautious not to see the distinction between normative and empirical legitimacy as too rigid, as a theorist is not only an observer but also a real-world actor.

Representative Legitimacy

From the classical era to the 17th century, democracy was largely associated with a gathering of citizens in assemblies or public meetings.[48] However, in the early 19th century, democracy began to be thought as the right of citizens take part in the determination of collective will through the election of representatives.[49] The idea of representative democracy was grounded in the work of liberal philosophers, such as James Madison and Jeremy Bentham, who were critics of direct democracy but argued for citizen empowerment to appoint their own rulers. With universal suffrage, liberal representative democracy took on its distinctive form, encompassing a cluster of rights and institutions such as elected government, free elections, and freedom of conscience, expression and information.[50]

Central to representative democracy is the idea that consent, expressed through the medium of election, legitimizes political power. In other words, the government's decisions and actions are legitimate if they represent the consent of the majority of the *demos*. To be sure, most modern representative democracies allow the elected representatives to delegate some of their powers to others, such as administrative agencies. However, the chain of authority that derives from democratic mechanisms—namely, election—imbues delegates with legitimacy as well.[51]

While the theory of representative democracy can fairly easily legitimize national governments, its application causes challenges at the supranational level. Indeed, supranational governance regimes might be regarded as illegitimate when they are seen through the lens of representative democracy. Absence of election and extensive chains of delegation are important reasons

48 Held, *supra* note 46 at 9–12.

49 *Ibid.*

50 *Ibid.*

51 *Ibid.*; Ilter Turan, "Democracy, Types of" in Bertrand Badie, Dirk Berg-Schlosser & Leonardo Morlino, eds, *International Encyclopaedia of Political Science* (Thousand Oaks, Cal: Sage Publications, 2011) at 592.

that representative democracy advocates make an argument for the unfeasibility of democracy at the international level.[52]

It must be conceded that direct election of international officials is unlikely in the near future. However, this unlikelihood need not end the discussion of legitimacy or legitimization at the global level. Indeed, emphasis on election or majority voting as the central institution of democracy has been regarded as misplaced. As Barker puts it:

> If democracy as a feature of government entails that policies, or rulers, reflect the wishes of the people or majority of them, then it could be achieved by responsive despotism or by authoritarian government informed by market research. It is paradoxically, such an account of democracy on which rational choice theory has concentrated while at the same time insisting on its impossibility.[53]

In short, it does not seem that majority voting or direct electoral underpinnings are essential prerequisites of legitimate governance. Decision-making procedures of international institutions could be designed so that they connect citizens to policymakers and engage them in a dialogue that establishes some degree of democratic legitimacy. The following will present such a topic.

Deliberative Legitimacy

In an early and very influential paper, Bernard Manin observes that, similar to liberalism, modern democratic thought is based on principles of individualism.[54] While there are differences between liberal and democratic points of view, both arrive at the same consideration of unanimity as the true source of legitimacy.[55] Basing political legitimacy on unanimity derives from the principles of modern individualism. By nature, individuals are free and equal

---

52 Diversity of interests and values at the global scale, lack of interest or knowledge of many citizens to involve in international issues are also reasons that have been mentioned in this his regard. See Robert A. Dahl, "Can International Organizations be Democratic? A Skeptic's View" in Ian Shapiro & Casiano Hacker-Cordón, eds, Democracy's edges (New York: Cambridge University Press, 1999).

53 Rodney Barker, "Democratic Legitimation: What Is It, Who Wants It, and Why?" in Achim Hurrelmann, Steffen Schneider & Jens Steffek, ed, *Legitimacy in an age of global politics* (New York: Palgrave Macmillan, 2007) 19 at 24.

54 Bernard Manin, "On Legitimacy and Political Deliberation" (1987) 15:3 *Political Theory* 338 at 341.
Ibid., at 340.

55 *Ibid.*, at 341.

to one another. There is no essential difference or natural hierarchy among individuals that can justify the domination of some over others. Since political power and the rules it promulgates bear on and constrain all members of society, they are legitimate as long as they arise from and represent the will of all.[56] At the same time, however, most democratic theories are not only concerned with legitimacy but also with efficiency. Such theories therefore bring into play the majority principle, which is a more realistic mechanism for decision making.[57] As a result, the question arises how 'unanimity'—as the principle of legitimacy—can be reconciled with 'majority'—the principle of decision making.

The work of Emmanuel Sieyès, the French political theorist, is remarkably illustrative of how liberal philosophers contemplated this question.[58] Sieyès posits that humans are free by nature; when they form a society or association, "only relations based on the free act of will of each individual can be established among them."[59] In his view, the laws of a society are legitimate only if they represent the achievement of unanimous will of all of its individuals.[60]

Sieyès acknowledges "unanimity being a very difficult objective to attain even among a rather small group of people," thus making it "impossible in a society of several million individuals."[61] With good reason then, majority becomes a substitute for unanimity. However, due to the centrality of unanimity as the true source of legitimacy in Sieyès's theory, he cannot dispose of it. Instead, he tries to transubstantiate majority into unanimity, asserting that one must resolve to find all the attributes of the former in the latter.[62] Sieyès' attempt is, of course, unsuccessful, as the will of the majority and the will of *all* are by no means equivalent. The word "majority" itself implies a degree of exclusion. However, it successfully illustrates the extreme difficulty that democratic theories face in reconciling unanimity—as the main source of legitimacy—with the practical realities of modern life.[63]

It should be noted that under the liberal democratic theories discussed above, the will of individuals that make collective decision making legitimate

56 *Ibid.*, at 340.

57 *Ibid.*

58 Emmanuel Sieyes, Vuessur les moyensd'exécutiondont les représentants de la France pourront disposer en 1979 (Pans, 1789), 15, cited in Manin, *ibid.*, at 365.

59 *Ibid.*

60 *Ibid.*

61 *Ibid.*

62 *Ibid.*

63 Manin, *supra* note 54 at 342.

is predetermined. In other words, such theories assume that an individual already knows what he or she wants when he or she comes to a public assembly, along with others, to assert a decision. Based on this assumption, deliberation becomes unnecessary, or even undesirable, because individuals have already made up their mind and any act of persuasion attempted by others could taint or oppress their will. Jean-Jacques Rousseau's *Social Contract* clearly makes such a point:

> Whenever men who have gathered together, consider themselves as one single body, they will have only one will, dedicated to the preservation of the community, and the general well-being. Then all the actions of the state would be vigorous and simple, its maxims clear and luminous. There will be no tangled, contradictory interests, the public good would be evident everywhere, and would only need common sense to be apprehended. Peace, unity, and equality are the enemies of political subtleties.[64] [Emphasis added]

Rousseau assumes that deliberation is unnecessary because citizens can independently make their own choices and the common good of a society is obvious. It is this assumption, however, that deliberative theorists characterize as the chief shortcoming of modern democratic thought. As Manin notes, the complexity of social life does not allow individuals to avail themselves of complete information. It is unreasonable to assume that individuals are already informed and have a complete set of preferences regarding a multitude of issues. They may only have incomplete and fragmentary knowledge of a problem or a solution. Deliberation could therefore be characterized as a procedure of becoming informed, allowing individuals to confront various points of view, clarify their information, and sharpen their preferences.[65] The significance of this procedure explains why the deliberative account argues for radical alteration of a perspective common to both liberal theories and democratic thought: legitimacy's source is not the predetermined will of individuals but the process of its formation—namely, deliberation.

Cohen observes that "the notion of deliberative democracy is rooted in the intuitive ideal of a democratic association in which the justification of terms and conditions of association proceeds through a public argument

64 Jean-Jacques Rousseau, *Du Contrat Social*, Book IV, chap. 1, 437, cited in Manin, *supra* note 54 at 346–347.

65 *Ibid.*, at 352.

and reasoning among equal citizens."[66] In such an order, citizens commit to the resolution of collective problems through public reasoning and consider their institutions legitimate insofar as they establish a framework for public deliberation.[67]

Central to the deliberative account of democracy are *reasoning* and *publicity*. In a deliberative account, reasons, rather than preference, constitute the main input into the democratic decision-making process. Reasons might be directed on policy proposals (what needs to be done) on the one hand, and the empirical claims and hypotheses on which proposals rest on the other. In most cases, participants in the deliberation do not agree on the reasons. Indeed, disagreement about the reasons for and against a course of action and evaluation of the conflicting reasons is the *raison d'être* of the deliberative process. The second dimension (publicity) requires deliberation participants to justify the reasons for which they prefer a particular course of action. Such justification is then scrutinized by other discussants. Indeed, as Fabienne Peter argues publicity is not only about the forum in which reasoning takes place, public deliberation vis-à-vis private deliberation, but also refers to the types of reasons given. A reason is public when it has the potential to be accepted by those who do not share the same point of view.[68]

The deliberative process is brought to an end by a choice. The proposal that wins the greatest support among participants will be adopted. However, the final decision is not legitimate simply because it carries the approval of the greatest number. Instead, it is legitimate because it is the outcome of a deliberative process where participants had the opportunity to voice their views and choose or refute a solution.[69]

Theories of deliberative democracy offer insights that prove useful when looking at the legitimacy of supranational governance arrangements. Arguably, a global governance regime carries greater legitimacy when its decision-making procedures are accompanied by an established framework for deliberation among different perspectives. Affected constituencies are more likely to grant an institution the right to rule when the institution gives reasons for its decisions and welcomes a public debate on the merit of such reasons. It is even arguable that an appropriate deliberative mechanism could substitute for democratic mechanisms, such as election, that are absent internationally.

---

66 Joshua Cohen, "Deliberation and Democratic Legitimacy" in James Bohman& William Rehg, *Deliberative Democracy: Essays on Reason and Politics* (MIT Press, 1997) 67 at 72.

67 *Ibid.*

68 Fabienne Peter, *Democratic legitimacy* (New York: Routledge, 2009) at 31–33.

69 Manin, *supra* note 54 at 359–360.

When designing a deliberative framework, attention must be given to the efficiency dimension of international policymaking. Deliberation should not unreasonably slow down or impose excessive costs on the decision-making process.

Rules-based Legitimacy

In his seminal volume, *The Morality of Law*, Lon Fuller exposes his view on the normative characteristics of a legal system.[70] Through the parable of *Rex* (the imaginary king and lawmaker), Fuller demonstrates several ways a legal regime may flounder, including failure to publicize rules, abusive use of retroactive rules, failure to make rules understandable, enactment of contradictory rules, rules impossible to implement, frequent changes to the rules so that action in accordance with them cannot be oriented, and failure of the rules to correspond to their interpretation or implementation. According to Fuller, the entire legal system may cease to be characterized as a legal system if it fails too extensively in any of these particularities.[71]

Interaction between rules and legitimacy at the international level has also been studied by legal scholars, including Thomas Franck. In his book, *Power of Legitimacy Among Nations*,[72] Franck rejects the view that an international norm or rule is legitimate when a coercive authority backs it. Instead, he argues that a rule is legitimate when those it addresses perceive the rule to be legitimate.[73] That is, they perceive the rule to have come into being and that it operates according to the right process. A full discussion of what Franck considers to be the right process is beyond the purview of this project; it suffices to say that the two main components of the right process of relevance to this contribution are determinacy and coherence.

A rule is determinate when its content can be ascertained with relative ease and certainty. Logically, rules that have a high degree of determinacy are more likely to be successful in regulating conduct than those that are less determinate because those to whose conduct the rules are directed can understand what is expected of them. This understanding is the first essential step toward compliance. In contrast, the more indeterminate a rule, the easier it is to justify

70 Lon L. Fuller, *The Morality of Law* (New Haven: Yale University Press, 1964).

71 *Ibid.*, at 33–94; Perry Meyer, Book Review of *Morality of Law* by Lon L. Fuller, (1964) 10 McGill LJ 380 at 381.

72 Thomas M. Franck, *The power of legitimacy among nations* (New York: Oxford University Press, 1990).

73 *Ibid.*, at 16.

non-compliance.[74] Franck recognizes that some degree of complexity and vagueness might be necessary for some rules.[75] An example, he offers *pacta sunt servanda*, which essentially means that treaties are binding. While this rule communicates a very clear message, its application may lead to problems. For instance, what if the subject matter of a treaty ceases to exist? What if the conditions in which a treaty operates change so dramatically that the application becomes irrational? Insistence on the implementation of the treaty in such circumstances produces absurd outcomes. International law therefore imposes the *clausula rebus sic stantibus*, which permits a treaty to be voided upon a profound change of circumstances.[76] Although *clausula rebus sic stantibus* reduces the clarity of *pacta sunt servanda*, it also prevents it from creating absurd outcomes. Franck, however, stresses that rules such as *clausula rebus sic stantibus* should not give states the license to do whatever they wish. Instead, there should be a legitimate interpretative process that allows for the case-by-case application of such rules.[77]

Another important way that rules can contribute to legitimacy is by coherence. Franck's conception of coherence is very similar to, and in fact draws upon, Ronald Dworkin's theory of integrity. Dworkin contends that integrity is helpful in understanding why rules are treated as compelling. He uses the term in two different, but related, fashions: *moral integrity*, which requires a rule to be principally related to the other rules of the same system, and *adjudicative integrity*, which means that all like cases will be treated alike in the application of a rule.[78] Using the same mode of analysis, Franck introduces two concepts of *coherence* and *consistency*. Similar to adjudicative integrity, consistency simply means treating likes alike. Coherence, however, which is of more significance, means that a rule is based on principles that are widely accepted (or at least not unacceptable) in the international community. Coherence legitimates a rule by providing a connection between the rule or its application on one hand, and its own principled purpose plus a web of other principles, including those previously used in similar cases, on the other hand.[79]

This brief introduction to some rule theories by jurisprudence scholars suggests that the legitimacy of any governance system, be it national or

74 *Ibid.*, at 50–52, 64–66.

75 *Ibid.*, at 84.

76 *Ibid.*, at 84–85.

77 *Ibid.*

78 Ronald Dworkin, *Law's Empire* (Cambridge, MA: Belknap Press of Harvard University Press, 1986) at 176–224; Franck, *supra* note 72 at 143.

79 Franck, *supra* note 72 at 143–149.

supranational, derives at least partially from having decision-making procedures and rules that are publicized, intelligible and coherent. The order and stability established by rules significantly contributes to good governance by preventing chaos and promoting collective action. In addition, Fuller's observation holds true in any context of governance in that one cannot be legitimately expected to comply with a rule when the rule is kept secret, cannot be understood, is contradicted by another rule, demands the impossible, or changes too often.

Outcome-based Legitimacy

Legitimacy may derive from the technical expertise of the governing institution and its ability to deliver socially beneficial outcomes. Theories of output legitimacy usually focus on the performance and accomplishment of an institution, rather than on its institutional characteristics. In other words, it is the institution's success in producing desirable outcomes that legitimizes its authority.[80] For instance, Bressman observes that "an institution derives legitimacy from its ability to solve problems that could not be addressed by other means."[81] Buchanan and Keohane similarly note that "the legitimacy of an institution is called into question if there is an institutional alternative, providing significantly greater benefits, that is feasible, accessible without excessive transition costs, and meets the minimal moral acceptability criterion."[82] Legitimacy based on outcomes has also been considered by Max Weber. Weber valued bureaucratic governance mainly because it allows delegation to experts whose knowledge, neutrality and insulation from politics promise delivery of superior policy outcomes.[83] Outcomes undoubtedly contribute to legitimacy; constituencies are more likely to recognize the authority of an institution when it delivers material objectives. For instance, the Basel Committee is perceived to be more legitimate to the extent that its policies help reduce the likelihood of financial crises and increase financial stability. It is also true that expertise is an essential condition for desirable institutional performance and a key reason for national governments to delegate authority to international institutions.

---

80 Chris Brummer, *Soft law and the Global Financial System: Rule Making in the 21st Century* (New York: Cambridge University Press, 2012) at 180.

81 *Ibid.*

82 Allen Buchanan & Robert O. Keohane, "The legitimacy of global governance institutions" (2006) 20:4 *Ethics and International Affairs* 405 at 405.

83 Max Weber, *Economy and Society: An Outline of Interpretive Society* (Berkley: University of Californian Press, 1978) at 216–227; Daniel C. Esty, "Good Governance at the Supranational Scale: Globalizing Administrative Law" (2006) 115 *Yale Law Journal* 1490 at 1517.

Two notes of caution are warranted here. First, technical performance is only one source of legitimacy, and while it is important, it does not eliminate the need for other substantive foundations of legitimacy. Indeed, some authors have argued that technical performance on its own cannot secure legitimacy. For instance, Jan Scholte observes that many constituencies have not treated the G8 as a legitimate institution, despite the material benefits that flow from its initiatives, including enhancing financial stability, combating climate change and broadening digital access.[84] Such perception is largely due to the fact that the G8 has extremely poor democratic credentials for a global authority, a problem that the shift to the G20 seeks to address. Similarly, the Group of Thirty may have significant expertise in economic and financial policy analysis, but because it lacks any constitutional or democratic grounds, few constituencies accord it with the right to rule.[85] Thus, global governance institutions must acquire legitimacy through a combination of grounds. Technocratic efficiency on its own does not generate sufficient support from the stakeholders[86] to sustain a regime.

Second, outcomes cannot be considered in isolation from the institution delivering them. The previous paragraphs explained how appropriate deliberative mechanisms and sound rulemaking can contribute to greater legitimacy. Such mechanisms can also positively affect the outcomes institutions produce. Giving voice to different perspectives and critically evaluating them helps institutions produce better policies. Likewise, institutions that operate based on a clear, stable rule system are more likely to find success, in contrast to a regime that operates based on incoherent and ambiguous rules.

Global Governance of Banking from the Lens of Global Administrative Law

The previous paragraphs developed the taxonomy of legitimacy, drawing upon four established bases for the acceptance of a governing authority: 1) majority will and representation, 2) dialogue and deliberation, 3) stability and coherence of rules, and 4) expertise and competence to generate material benefits. It illustrated that institutions of global governance often lack direct mechanisms of democracy, such as elections, at the national level. It was, however, argued that the regimes of global governance could be further legitimized by

84 Jan A. Scholte, "Global Governance, Accountability, and Civil Society" in Jan A. Scholte, ed, *Building Global Democracy: Civil Society and Accountable Global Governance* (New York: Cambridge University Press, 2011) 8 at 114–115 [Scholte, "Global Governance and Accountability"].

85 *Ibid.*

86 For the definition of stakeholders see the discussion of accountability below.

nurturing other accepted bases of legitimacy, such as appropriate deliberation mechanisms or governance through sound and stable rules. Against such a background, the following paragraphs will elaborate further on the approach and principles of my project upon evaluation of the legitimacy of the global governance of banking.

Global administrative law (GAL) is the basic theoretical framework used in my project. GAL is an emerging field that refers to "mechanisms, principles, practices, and supporting social understandings that promote or otherwise affect the accountability of global administrative bodies, in particular by ensuring they meet adequate standards of transparency, participation, reasoned decision, and legality, and by providing effective review of the rules and decisions they make."[87]

As noted by Benedict Kingsbury, Nico Krisch, and Richard Stewart, underlying GAL's emergence is the vast increase in the types and reach of transnational regulation and administration. Today, global interdependencies in such fields as security, development, environmental protection, banking, intellectual property and trade give rise to pressing issues that cannot be addressed by isolated national measures. As a result, various transnational systems of regulation and cooperation have been established that take on many important regulatory functions of national regimes. In light of this, GAL offers two important insights. First, much of what is termed "global governance" can be accurately characterized as administrative action.[88] Many institutions and regimes that engage in global governance perform functions that have a genuine administrative character. That is to say, they operate below the level of treaty making but still manage and regulate vast aspects of social and economic life through specific decisions and rules. This is particularly the case with regard to transnational regulatory networks (TRN) such as the Basel Committee. From a legal point of view, the TRN's function can be distinguished from both legislation in the form of treaty making and adjudication in the form of dispute settlement (between states or other disputing parties). Second, administrative action performed by various governance regimes could be regulated by administrative law-type principles, rules and mechanisms.[89] The case for such regulation arises because these institutions, unlike their national counterparts, are not

87 Benedict Kingsbury, Nico Krisch & Richard B. Stewart, "The Emergence of Global Administrative Law" (2005) 68:15 Law & Contemp Probs 15 at 17.

88 *Ibid.*

89 *Ibid.*

subject to direct control by national governments or domestic legal systems. This situation creates an accountability deficit that GAL seeks to address.[90]

It is important to note that GAL's principles and standards are broad enough to be applied to a multitude of global governance regimes, including formal governmental regulatory bodies, informal intergovernmental regulatory networks, and hybrid public–private or private transnational bodies. There are, of course, important differences among these regimes. Some of them merely provide a framework for state action, whereas others establish guidelines that directly address domestic administrative agencies. Some regulatory regimes have their own enforcement mechanisms, while others may simply rely on national authorities to implement the rules. Nevertheless, such differences do not constitute a barrier to GAL's application given that GAL does not focus on specificities of the substantive rules generated by these institutions, but on the existence and operation of a minimum set of good governance principles that are intended to ensure legality, transparency and accountability.[91]

Sources of Global Administrative Law

An important question that arises asks where the norms and principles of GAL come from. As the following paragraphs will demonstrate, there is no definitive answer to this question. GAL is a new field whose principles, domain and sources are still under development. The written instruments concerning its norms are scattered and the practices of global administrative bodies are fragmented. Disagreement seems inevitable about whose practices to rely on for rules and how much consistency in practice is needed to generate adhesion.

However, such issues may seem less challenging in light of the fact that a legal commonality could be imposed on diverse norms and practices that GAL builds upon. As Benedict Kingsbury notes:

> ... the various mechanisms for accountability, for participation, and for the strengthening ... legitimacy in these different governance structures are evolving not simply in parallel but in increasingly interconnected ways that represent an emerging global administrative law.[92]

The following paragraphs will consider GAL's sources under two broad categories: national and transnational.

90 *Ibid.*, at 16–18.

91 *Ibid.*, at 17, 20–23.

92 Benedict Kingsbury, "The Administrative Law Frontier in Global Governance" (2005) 99 Am Soc'y Int'l L Proc 143 at 148.

National Sources

The primary function of administrative law in domestic legal systems is control of public power. Administrative law subjects administrative agencies to the rule of law and prescribes behaviours within their organization. As the authors of a leading administrative law text write:

> Administrative law is the law relating to the control of governmental power. This, at any rate, is the heart of the subject as viewed by most lawyers.... The primary purpose of administrative law is therefore to keep the powers of government within their legal bounds, so as to protect the citizen against their abuse. The powerful engines of authority must be prevented from running amok.[93]

This characterization reflects the fact that the main systems of administrative law established themselves in the context of constitutions that placed great emphasis on the separation of powers. *Marbury v. Madison*[94] in United States and *Prince Napleon*[95] in France were early precedents that established judicial control over acts previously considered governmental or apolitical. In other words, these cases illustrate the role that administrative law played in the struggle for limited government.[96]

In most systems, administrative law has evolved mainly as a system of principles with significant procedural characteristics. Administrative law requires the government to stay within the boundaries of legality or, in the parlance of US administrative law, not to overstep their power as delegates. Out of such boundaries originates the principle of legality central to all administrative law systems, known as *ultra vires* in Common Law and *excès de pouvoir* in civil law France.[97] Legality requires the administration to act within its powers and observe the principles of due process.

As Shapiro puts it, administrative law contains "a set of rules prescribing the proper rule-making behaviour for administrative agencies; that is,

93 William Wade & Christopher Forsyth, *Administrative Law*, 10th ed (New York: Oxford University Press, 2009) at 4.

94 *Marbury v. Madison*, 1 Cranch 137, 2 L Ed 60 (1803).

95 Conseild'Etat, 19 Feb. 1875, Prince Napoléon, Rec. 155, concl. David.

96 Carol Harlow, "Global Administrative Law: The Quest for Principles and Values" (2006) 17:1 EJIL 182 at 191.

97 *Ibid.*

administrative law is a key set of procedures."[98] Common examples of such procedural rules include public notification of proposed rules and inviting interested parties to comment, providing opportunities for public participation, giving reasons for decisions, and providing mechanisms for review and correction.[99] These procedural rules are arguably associated with broader principles such as openness, rationality and accountability, all of which promote the ideal of good governance according to law.[100] This section will return to that topic later.

Transnational Sources

GAL's formal transnational sources are classic sources of public international law, namely treaties, custom and general principles. It is, however, important to note that such sources do not always account for GAL's origins and the authority of normative practice that already exists in the field. For instance, treaties may rarely address issues of administrative law, and when they do they are addressed to states and not to international organizations or transnational networks. Similarly, international customary law has been mainly forged by state action and does not incorporate practices of non-state actors. The acceptance of general principles in international law has also been low and limited to norms that are subject to a high degree of worldwide convergence. It therefore seems unlikely that general principles will be extended to the diverse and fragmented context of global administration.[101]

Accordingly, the limitations of formal transnational sources suggest that while GAL is influenced by treaties and international customary law, it goes beyond such sources and, in some cases, may even move away from them. What is important is that GAL builds on the existing and emerging normative practices of global institutions, regardless of whether or not their governance or administrative functions originate from classic sources of international law. Mapping and exploring all such practices is beyond the scope of this contribution. By way of example, however, this section will review the practices of three institutions central to the global governance of security, trade and finance.

98 Martin Shapiro, "The Institutionalization of European Administrative Space" in Alec S. Sweet, Wayne Sandholtz, & Neil Fligstein, eds, *The Institutionalisation of Europe* (New York: Oxford University Press, 2001) 94 at 94.

99 Kingsbury, *supra* note 92 at 146.

100 Mark I. Aronson, Bruce Douglas Dyer & Matthew Groves, *Judicial Review of Administrative Action*, 3rd ed (Pyrmont, NSW: Lawbook Co, 2004) at 1.

101 Kingsbury, Krisch & Stewart, *supra* note 87 at 29.

UN Security Council Delisting Procedures

Under Chapter VII of the United Nations Charter, the Security Council can take measures to maintain or restore international peace and security.[102] Such measures can include acting directly on individuals through targeted sanctions and the associated listing of persons deemed to pose threats to international peace. Such targeted sanctions can involve freezing of assets or blocking of financial transactions.[103] In 2006, the Security Council adopted Resolution 1730, which sought to review delisting requests from targeted persons.[104] In 2009, Resolution 1904 allowed "individuals, groups, undertakings or entities seeking to be removed from the Security Council's Al-Qaida Sanctions Committee List" to submit their request for delisting to "an independent and impartial ombudsperson" appointed by the Secretary-General.[105] The delisting procedure was adopted, in part, in response to domestic court reviews of listing decisions.[106] While it may seem limited in nature, it incorporates some elements of reasoned decision making and review into the work of Security Council. Thus, it illustrates GAL's insight that an internal accountability mechanism can help enhance the legitimacy of an institution.[107]

World Bank Inspection Panel

The Inspection Panel was established by the International Bank for Reconstruction and Development (IBRD) and the International Development Association (IDA) in September 1993.[108] The establishing resolution allows

102 Under the UN Charter, the Security Council has primary responsibility for the maintenance of international peace and security. It has 15 members, and each member has one vote. Under the Charter, all state members must comply with Council decisions. See UN, "The Security Council" (Accessed on 25 April 2016) online: UN http://www.un.org/en/sc/

103 UNSC, "Security Council Sanctions Committees: An Overview" (Accessed on 25 April 2016) online: UN http://www.un.org/sc/committees/.

104 UNSC, "Focal Point for De-listing established pursuant to Security Council resolution 1730" (2006) online: http://www.un.org/sc/committees/dfp.shtml.

105 Office of the Ombudsperson, "An independent and Impartial Ombudsperson, Who Reviews Requests From Individuals, Groups, undertakings or Entities Seeking to be Removed from the Al-Qaida Sanctions List of the Security Council's Al-Qaida Sanctions Committee" (2013) online: UN http://www.un.org/en/sc/ombudsperson/ [Ombudsperson, "Delisting Requests"].

106 Peter Gutherie, "Security Council Sanctions and the Protection of Individual Rights" (2004) 60 NYU ANN SURV AM L 491 at 512–514.

107 Kingsbury, Krisch& Stewart, *supra* note 87 at 34.

108 Inspection Panel, "Panel Resolution and Mandate" (2013) online: World Bank http://web.worldbank.org/WBSITE/EXTERNAL/EXTINSPECTIONPANEL/0,,contentMDK:20173262~menuPK:64129254~pagePK:64129751~piPK:64128378~theSitePK:380794,00.html.

the panel jurisdiction over operations supported by the IBRID and IDA. The Inspection Panel provides a forum for people who have been adversely affected by bank-financed operations, to bring their concerns to the World Bank.[109] The Panel determines whether the World Bank is complying with its own policies and procedures that are intended to ensure that bank-financed operations provide benefits for communities and avoid social and environmental harm. The Panel consists of three members who are selected based on "their ability to deal thoroughly and fairly with the requests brought to them, their integrity and independence from Bank Management, and their exposure to developmental issues and living conditions in developing countries."[110]

What made the Panel unique at the time of its establishment, was that it allowed a group of two or more individuals to trigger the procedure and thereby established the first legally relevant relationship between individuals and an international institution.[111] In this respect, the Panel was the first international accountability mechanism of its kind and was fairly quickly emulated by other Multilateral Development Banks (MDBs).[112] As noted by some scholars, the structure and institution of the Panel suffers from shortcomings, Such as limited jurisdiction and inadequate authority.[113] Nevertheless, the standards and practices generated by the panel have been an important source of normative contribution toward enhancing the legitimacy and accountability of international institutions.

World Trade Organization

Article X of the 1947 General Agreement on Tariff and Trade (GATT) has been considered as the "oldest transparency and good governance obligation of the

---

109 *Ibid.*

110 Inspection Panel, "About Us" (2013) online: World Bank: http://web.worldbank.org/WBSITE/EXTERNAL/EXTINSPECTIONPANEL/0,,menuPK:64129249~pagePK:64132081~piPK:64132052~theSitePK:380794,00.html.

111 Ellen Hey, "The World Bank Inspection Panel: Towards the Recognition of a New Legally Relevant Relationship in International Law" (1997) 2 Hofstra L. & Pol'y Symp 61.

112 See for more information, Daniel D. Bradlow & Andria N. Fourie, "Independent Accountability Mechanisms at International and Regional Development Banks" in Thomase Hale & David Held, eds, *Handbook of Innovations in Transnational Governance* (Cambridge: Polity Press, 2011) 122.

113 See, e.g., Stephanie R. Roos, "The World Bank Inspection Panel in Its Seventh Year: An Analysis of Its Process, Mandate, and Desirability with Special Reference to the China (Tibet) Case" (2001) 5 *Max Planck Yearbook of United Nations Law* 473; Korinna Horta, "Rhetoric and Reality: Human Rights and the World Bank" (2002) 15 Harv Hum Rts J 227.

WTO."[114] This article imposes broad publication and due process requirements on the administration of trade measures, including the following:

> Laws, regulations, judicial decisions and administrative rulings related to trade issues (such as customs, duties and method of payment) must be "published promptly in such manner as to enable governments and traders to become acquainted with them."[115]

Such laws, regulations and decisions must be administered "in a uniform, impartial and reasonable manner."[116]

Members should establish judicial, arbitral or administrative tribunals or procedures for the purpose of review and correction of administrative actions related to custom matters. Such tribunals or procedures must be independent from agencies entrusted with administrative enforcement.[117]

An interesting analysis of Article X can be found in *United States—Restrictions on Imports of Cotton and Man-Made Fiber Underwear* (*United States—Underwear*)[118] where the WTO Appellate Body states:

> Article X: 2 ... may be seen to embody a principle of fundamental importance—that of *promoting full disclosure of governmental acts affecting Members and private persons and enterprises, whether of domestic or foreign nationality.* The relevant policy principle is widely known as the principle of transparency and has obvious due process dimensions. The essential implication is that Members and other persons affected, or likely to be affected, by governmental measures imposing restraints, requirements, and other burdens, should have a reasonable opportunity to acquire authentic information about such measures and accordingly

114 Padideh Ala'i, "From the Periphery to the Center? The Evolving WTO Jurisprudence on Transparency and Good Governance" (2008) 11:4 J Int'l Econ L 779 at 779.

115 *General Agreement on Tariffs and Trade*, 30 October 1947, 58 NTS 187, Can TS 1947 No. 27, art X [GATT] Please note that the language of Article X remains unchanged in GATT 1994. See WTO, "Legal texts: the WTO agreements" (2013) online: WTO http://www.wto.org/english/docs_e/legal_e/ursum_e.htm#General.

116 GATT, *ibid.*, art. X.

117 *Ibid.*

118 *United States—Restrictions on Imports of Cotton and Man-Made Fibre Underwear* (*United States—Underwear*) (1997) WTO/DS24/AB/R (Appellate Body Report) online: WTO http://www.wto.org/english/tratop_e/dispu_e/ab_reports_e.htm.

> to protect and adjust their activities or alternatively to seek modification of such measures ... [emphasis added][119]

The importance of Article X was underscored again in *Import Prohibition of Certain Shrimp and Shrimp Products* (*US—Shrimp*).[120] At issue was whether the US import ban of shrimp and shrimp products could be justified under the General Exceptions in Article XX of GATT. The Appellate Body stated that Article X:3 could help interpret Article XX because it "establishes certain minimum standards for transparency and procedural fairness in the administration of trade regulations."[121] It was held that the ban would not qualify as an exception because the US government denied basic fairness and due process" to foreign governments applying for certification under the US shrimp–turtle regulation.[122]

This brief discussion of Article X and its surrounding jurisprudence suggests that transparency has become a central principle in the WTO regime. In addition to its importance as a benchmark for the review of domestic administrative decisions by WTO tribunals, the principle of transparency channels and disciplines the global trade regulation. Taken together, the three example considered here demonstrate how a global regulatory regime can be held accountable to norms of administrative law character.

Criteria for Assessment of Legitimacy

The assessment my project makes on the legitimacy of the global governance of banking will be guided by three overarching principles: reasoning, transparency and accountability. These principles have been the subject of a rich debate in legal scholarship, and in GAL in particular. Drawing upon such debate, the following paragraphs elaborate on the three principles and illustrate how they affect and operate in domestic and international settings. Yet, it is crucial to note that the reach and significance of these principles transcend any given doctrine, be it in jurisprudence, political science, or any other discipline. Most scholars who are concerned with normative legitimacy seem to agree that a system of governance cannot be legitimate unless it operates transparently, provides reasons for its decisions, and remains accountable to those it affects.

---

119 *Ibid.*, at 21.

120 *United States—Measures Relating to Shrimp from Thailand* (2008) WT/DS343/R (Appellate Body Report) online: WTO http://www.wto.org/english/tratop_e/dispu_e/ab_reports_e.htm.

121 *Ibid.*, at para 183.

122 *Ibid.*, at para 181.

For example, reference can be made to "Global Governance and Legitimacy" where Robert Keohane identifies transparency as a crucial criterion in the evaluation of legitimacy. Keohane argues that the ability of the ruled to control the ruler depends on their access to information about the ruler's behaviour.[123] Keohane also considers accountability as another important standard of legitimacy. In his view, accountability provides the ruled with power over the ruler, and is comprised of three important elements: 1) standards that are expected to be met by those who are held accountable; 2) information that is made available to accountability holders, enabling them to apply the standards in question to those who are held accountable; and 3) the ability of the accountability holders to impose sanctions when there is a failure in meeting the standards.[124]

Reference can be also made to Jens Steffek's scholarship, which is illustrative of the significance of reason giving.[125] Drawing upon Max Weber's idea of rational legal domination and on Jürgen Habermas's idea of legitimation through justificatory discourse, Steffek argues that the legitimacy of an international governance regime hinges upon its success in justifying its goals, principles and procedures.[126] He notes that whereas in pre-modern times legitimacy was mainly derived from divine authority, modern legitimacy is derived from authority of reason. Reason giving is the communicative process that legitimates governance.[127]

One must keep in mind that the principles discussed here are interrelated and the boundaries among them maybe considerably blurred. For instance, as will be explained further below, transparency can be considered a precondition of accountability. Similarly, an institution cannot be perceived as legitimate when it does not even provide reasons for its actions. It is, therefore, plausible to consider these principles under different frameworks or classifications.

Finally, the principles that will be discussed below are chosen for their importance with regard to the global regime of banking, as well as for the broad agreement of their desirability. However, they are not by any means exhaustive of the criteria for legitimacy. Inclusiveness, fairness, impartiality, minimal

123 Robert O. Keohane, "Global Governance and Legitimacy" (2011) 18:1 *Review of International Political Economy* 99 at 101 [Keohane, "Global Governance and Legitimacy"].

124 *Ibid.*, at 102.

125 Jens Steffek, "Legitimation of International Governance: A Discourse Approach" (2003) 9 *European Journal of International Relations* 249.

126 *Ibid.*

127 *Ibid.*, at 263.

moral acceptability, epistemic quality and legality are some of the criteria used by scholars in their analysis of the legitimacy of global governance.[128]While the differences among these criteria are sometimes primarily about the terminology used, they can also be used to denote substantively different concepts. This theoretical question, however, falls outside the purview of this project.

Reasoning

Max Weber argues that bureaucracy is an efficient form of organization due to its rationality.[129] Bureaucratic decisions are not arbitrary manifestations of personal will. Instead, they are the outcome of reasoning. Weber says that "the only decisive point for us is that in principle a system of rationally debatable reasons stand behind every act of bureaucratic administration, namely either assumption under norms, or a weighing of ends and means."[130] Thus, bureaucratic authorities should give rational reasons for their actions and decisions.[131]

However, rational decision making cannot be based exclusively on reasons. Reasons must also be rationally debatable. The idea of rational debate implies that the decision maker and the stakeholders can meaningfully engage in a discussion about the reasons on which the decisions are based. As Steffek points out, communicability of reason "is the mechanism that enables individuals to exchange their views and communicatively to agree on strategies of action."[132]

Rational justification is an important source of legitimacy. An international institution can enhance its legitimacy by engaging in a rational dialogue with its stakeholders. Such a dialogue can help the institution justify its existence or, alternately, to partially or entirely reform its governance.

The importance of reasons as the basis for the legitimate exercise of power stands at the heart of administrative law. Here are a few examples of the duty of reason-giving in different legal systems:

---

128 For discussion and application of such criteria, see Keohane, "Global governance and legitimacy", *supra* note 123 at 101–108; Scholte, "Towards Greater Legitimacy", *supra* note 46 at 110–120; William D. Coleman & Tony Porter "International Institutions, Globalisation and Democracy: Assessing the Challenges" (2000) 14:3 *Global Society* 377; Esty, *supra* note 83 at 1515–1523.

129 Weber, *supra* note 83 at 979.

130 *Ibid.*

131 Steffek, *supra* note 125 at 261.

132 *Ibid.*, at 262.

- The *US Administrative Procedure Act*[133] requires administrative agencies to "incorporate in the rules adopted a concise general statement of their basis and purpose."[134]
- Under the *Netherlands' General Administrative Law Act*, administrative decisions must be based on valid reasons stated at the time a decision is disclosed.[135]
- Art. 39 (1) of the *German Administrative Procedure Act* (1976) provides that "An administrative act... shall be accompanied by a statement of grounds. This statement of grounds must contain the chief material and legal grounds that led the authority to take its decision. The grounds given in connection with discretionary decisions shall also contain the points of view which the authority considered while exercising its powers of discretion."[136]
- Article 3(1) of the Italian *Administrative Procedure Act* (1990) provides that "Save in the situations provided for under subsection (2), every administrative measure, including those regarding administrative organisation, personnel and the conduct of public competitive examinations, must include a statement of reasons. The statement of reasons must set out the factual premises and the points of law that determined the authority's decision, as these emerge from the preliminary fact-finding activities."[137]

From a legal perspective, the duty to give reasons seems to serve its purpose in three important ways. First, it enables the affected parties to know why a decision is adopted and on what factual and legal basis it is founded. Second, an obligation to state reasons motivates decisionmakers to diligently think through the rationale of their actions. As Craig notes, "having to explain oneself, and defend the rationality of one's choice, is always a salutary exercise."[138]

---

133 *Administrative Procedure Act*, 5 USC § 553(c) (2000) [USAPC].

134 USAPC, *ibid.*, § 556(e).

135 *General Administrative Law Code* (Algemene wet bestuursecht, AWB), Act of June 1992 in force on January 1994, Official Journal (Staatsblad) 1994, nr. A, arts 3:46–3:47 as cited in René Seerden & Frits Stroink, "Administrative Law in the Netherlands" in René Seerden & Frits Stroink (eds) *Administrative Law of the European Union, Its Member States and the United States: A Comparative Analysis* (Cambridge, UK: Intersentia, 2002) 145 at 147.

136 Unofficial translation available in the issue n. 2/2010 of the *Italian Journal of Public Law* (*www.ijpl.eu*). See for further detail, Giacinto della Cananea, 'The Giving Reasons Requirement: A Global Standard for Public Authorities" in Giacinto Della Cananea & Aldo Sandulli, *Global Standards for Public Authorities* (Editoriale Scientifica, 2012) at 14.

137 Unofficial translation published by the Federal Ministry of the Interior. See, Della Cananea, *ibid.*, at 14.

138 Paul P. Craig, *EU Administrative Law* (New York: Oxford University Press, 2006) at 382.

Third, the existence of reasons facilitates oversight—particularly judicial review—to determine if a decision was irrational or disproportionate.[139]

The principle to give reasons has been also extended from domestic law into some regional and global institutions. Article 253 of the Treaty Establishing the European Community (EC Treaty) provides the following:

> Regulations, directives and decisions adopted jointly by the European Parliament and the Council, and such acts adopted by the Council or the Commission, shall state the reasons on which they are based and shall refer to any proposals or opinions, which were required to be obtained pursuant to this Treaty.[140]

Similarly, The UN Security Council Sanction Committee is required to give reasons for placing individuals or entities on the sanctions list and provide a narrative summary of the case on its website. The summary should include the basis for listing according to relevant Security Council resolutions, as well as specific information demonstrating that the individual or entity meets the criteria for listing set out in the resolutions.[141] These examples show that reason giving is an important standard for public authorities and a requirement prevalent in many areas of global governance practice.

Transparency

In broad terms, transparency refers to the degree to which information is available to constituencies of a governance regime, enabling them to understand and assess the decisions made and have an informed voice in decision making.[142] Those who are affected must be able to discover what and when decisions are taken, by whom, and under what procedures. Without such information, constituencies are left ignorant and cannot effectively scrutinize the actor.[143]

---

139 *Ibid.*, at 382.

140 *Treaty Establishing the European Community (Nice consolidated version)*, 24 December 2002, Official Journal C 325, 24/12/2002 P. 0135–0135, online: EU http://eur-lex.europa.eu/LexUriServ/LexUriServ.do?uri=CELEX:12002E253:EN:HTML [EC Treaty]

141 Security Council Committee Pursuant to Resolutions 1267 (1999) and 1989 (2011) Concerning Al-Qaida and Associated Individuals and Entities, "Guidelines of the Committee for the Conduct of Its Work" (2013) at 12, online: UN http://www.un.org/sc/committees/1267/pdf/1267_guidelines.pdf.

142 Ann Florini, "The Battle over Transparency" in Ann Florini, ed, *The Right to Know: Transparency for an Open World* (New York: Columbia University Press, 2007) 1 at 5.

143 Scholte, "Global Governance and Accountability", *supra* note 84 at 16.

Transparency contributes to good governance in at least three ways. First, transparency makes accountability possible. Without free access to information, people have little chance of knowing, let alone having a say, in decisions that affect their lives. Second, transparency can address, or at least disclose, a host of principal-agency issues by shining light on decision makers' actions and deterring such decision makers from turning public service into a means of private gain. Finally, transparency is a key component of effective policy-making. Even the most competent decisionmakers need feedback on how the policies they have adopted are working in actual practice.[144]

Transparency has been the focus of administrative law in many jurisdictions. For instance the *US Administrative Procedure Act* requires administrative agencies to publish a notice of the proposed rulemaking in the Federal Registrar. The notice should include a statement of the time, place, and nature of the rulemaking,the legal authority under which the rule is proposed, and a description of the substance of the rule and the issues involved.[145]Administrative agencies are also required to make the following information available to public:

- A description of the organization and the methods whereby the public may obtain information, make submissions or requests, or obtain decisions;
- A statement of the general course and method by which its functions are channeled and determined, including the nature and requirements of its formal and informal procedures;
- A statement of general values and policies.[146]

Transnationally, transparency is deemed to be an important value. For instance, the Treaty on the European Union (EC Treaty) requires the Union's institutions and bodies to "conduct their work as openly as possible."[147] This requirement is intended to promote good governance and ensure the participation of civil society. The right to access EU documents has been also protected by the *EU Charter of Fundamental Rights*,[148] which asserts:

144 Florini, *supra* note 142 at 1–5.

145 UPAC § 553.

146 *Ibid.*; *Freedom of Information Act* 5 USC § 552 (1966).

147 EC Treaty, *supra* note 140, art. 15.

148 *Charter of Fundamental Rights of the European Union*, 18 December 2000, (2000/C 364/01) online: EU http://www.europarl.europa.eu/charter/default_en.htm [EU Charter].

> Any citizen of the Union, and any natural or legal person residing or having its registered office in a Member State, has a right of access to European Parliament, Council and Commission documents.[149]

Transparency has been enacted to the fullest extent in the founding documents and internal procedures of the WTO. Article X of GATT requires all WTO members to "publish [regulations] promptly in such a manner as to enable governments and traders to become acquainted with them".[150] The WTO uses web-based tools to give the public access to a variety of documents. In terms of notification of domestic regulation, the *Marrakesh Decision on Notification Procedures* affirmed pre-existing obligations and established a central registry for notification managed by the Secretariat.[151] In 2002, the WTO General Council's historic "transparency decision" established the rule that "all WTO official documents shall be unrestricted."[152] Practically speaking, this means that all decisions, meeting minutes, accession protocols, laws and regulations and Secretariat decisions are translated to the WTO's three official languages and then made public on the WTO website.

With respect to dispute settlement, document availability to the public depends on a specific stage of the process. The WTO promptly posts updates on the status of disputes and maintains a registry of all cases. When a member state makes a request for consultation,[153] the WTO issues a summary of the request, including a description of the contested measure, as well as the legal basis for the complaint. Actual consultations are held in camera but are not otherwise documented or released to the public. Should the consultation prove fruitless, a member can request the establishment of a panel to settle the dispute and the content of the request is published on the WTO website.

---

149 EU Charter, *ibid.*, art. 42.

150 GATT, *supra* note 115, art. X.

151 WTO, *Reports of the Subsidiary Bodies to the General Council for Trade in Goods* (1996) Vol. II, Annex 1 at 16–18, online: WTO http://www.wto.org/english/thewto_e/minist_e/min96_e/w46-2.pdf.

152 WTO, *Procedures for the Circulation and De-restriction of WTO Documents* (2002) T/L/452, online: WTO http://members.wto.org/WTO_resources/documentation/derestriction_e.htm.

153 Consultation is the first stage of a formal dispute settlement. It gives the parties the opportunity to discuss the matter and find a satisfactory solution without resorting to litigation. See WTO, "The Process—Stages in a Typical WTO Dispute Settlement Case" online: WTO http://www.wto.org/english/tratop_e/dispu_e/disp_settlement_cbt_e/c6s2p1_e.htm.

Panel and Appellate body decisions are also available to the public after their adoption.[154]

Accountability

Accountability is an essential condition for the establishment and maintenance of legitimate and effective global governance. In the absence of accountability, there are major deficits in the provision of global public goods, such as ecological integrity, financial stability, and disease control. Across the diverse and contrasting conceptions that exist with regard to accountability, "there is general agreement that accountability is a condition and process whereby an actor answers for its conduct to those whom it affects".[155] This statement could be illustrated by a simple example. If A takes an action that affects B, then under the principle of accountability A must answer to B for that action and its consequences. Accountability is therefore linked to power: if A has the power to affect B, it has also a duty to account for the exercising of its power.[156] Determining to whom accountability should be made available is a challenging task, but as the definition used here suggests, the key test seems to be "affected interest".[157] Accordingly, a global governing institution is accountable to those whose lives and affairs it influences. Those people affected by an institution's actions collectively form that institution's constituency.[158] With regard to global banking governance, this means that constituencies comprise not only domestic regulators but also countries, and especially in the sense of countries' citizens. Citizens ultimately bear the weighty consequences of banking crises that regulations fail to prevent, in terms of losing jobs, homes, and funding bailouts.

Accountability can be understood to have prospective and retrospective aspects. Prospective aspects of accountability are transparency and consultation. Transparency, which requires an actor to be visible to affected constituencies,

---

154 Gabrielle Marceau & Mikella Hurley, "Transparency and Public Participation in the WTO: A Report Card on WTO Transparency Mechanisms" (2012) 4:1 TRADE L & DEV 19 at 25–26.

155 Scholte, "Global Governance and Accountability", *supra* note 84 at 16.

156 International Law Association, *Accountability of International Organizations* (2004) at 5, online: ILA. http://www.ila-hq.org/download.cfm/docid/6B708C25-4D6D-42E2-8385DADA752815E8 [ILA].

157 Erika D. Wet, "Holding International Institutions Accountable: The Complementary Role of Non-Judicial Oversight Mechanisms and Judicial Review" in Armin V. Bogdandy et al., eds, *The Exercise of Public Authority by International Institutions: Advancing International Institutional Law* (New York: Springer, 2010) 855 at 858.

158 Scholte, "Global Governance and Accountability", *supra* note 84 at 21.

was discussed to some length in the preceding paragraphs. With respect to consultation, accountability requires a decision maker to explain its actions to affected constituencies and incorporate those constituencies in deliberation and allow them to shape outcomes.[159]

Retrospective elements of accountability broadly fall into two categories: evaluation and correction. With respect to evaluation, accountability requires the actor's action, and its impact on affected parties, to be subject to independent oversight and assessment. With respect to correction, accountability requires that affected constituencies be provided with redress in cases where the affecting actor has made wrong decisions with harmful consequences.[160]

The different dimensions of accountability alluded to above can be found in various forms, and to varying degrees, at the domestic level. Many legislatures have promulgated rules requiring administrative bodies (particularly regulatory agencies) to provide information allowing legislatures to monitor and assess their actions, policies and procedures. Regulators are often required to publish reports that explain the basis of their decision making and to inform the public on rules they intend to pass or implement. On some occasions, public hearings are required or third party observers are allowed to attend meetings.[161] Finally, administrative decisions are subject to judicial review. If an administrative agency renders its decision in bad faith or exceeds the jurisdiction granted, the court will deem the decision to have no effect. The court will also nullify a decision that is improper with regard to the policy objectives established by the agency (decision made for *improper purposes*), or one that is based on irrelevant considerations (decisions *in abuse of power*).[162]

As a general rule, direct instruments of accountability that operate on the domestic level are absent at the supranational level. As previously stated, there is no global legislative assembly that can provide a direct link between the governed and the governors. Global governance also lacks judicial proceedings through which affected parties can seek evaluation and correction of flawed regulatory policies. While courts with global jurisdiction do exist—such as the International Court of Justice (ICJ)—they do not adjudicate on the conduct of TRN.[163]

---

159 *Ibid.*, at 16–17.

160 *Ibid.*, at 41.

161 Brummer, *supra* note 80 at 185–186.

162 Gerald L. Gall, *The Canadian legal system*, 5th ed (Ont.: Carswell, 2004) at 549–550.

163 *Statute of the International Court of Justice*, art. 36, online: ICJ http://www.icj-cij.org/documents/index.php?p1=4&p2=2&p3=0.

Nevertheless, the absence of a domestic mechanism of accountability does not remove potential for a suitably accountable global regulatory regime. Some useful insights in this respect could be derived from the three-layered model of accountability provided by the International Law Association (ILA).[164] The first level of accountability in this model concerns the extent to which an international institution, in fulfillment of its functions, is subject to forms of scrutiny and monitoring, regardless of potential and subsequent liability in a legal sense.[165] The second level of accountability is concerned with tortious liability for injurious consequences of acts and omissions that do not involve a breach of any rule of international law. A good example of this type of liability is environmental damage arising out of lawful nuclear or space activity. The third level of liability arises out of acts or omissions that constitute a breach of international or institutional law. Examples of the third level include violations of human rights, gross negligence and breach of contract, or as far as institutional law is concerned, acts of organs that are *ultra vires* or violate the law of employment relations.[166]

Whereas the second and third levels of accountability correspond to classic legal notions of state responsibility as well as responsibility of international organizations, the first level, which is of greater significance to this project, is considerably broader. It encompasses a range of non-judicial procedures for scrutinizing the behaviour of international institutions. Further, it is applicable to both formal and informal international institutions, including TRN.[167]

Current practices of transnational institutions reflect the increasing significance of general oversight mechanisms. A common phenomenon is vertical oversight where the parent organization exercises formal supervision over a subsidiary organ. The oversight is characterized as vertical as there is a hierarchical relationship between the respective organs.[168] The parent has the right to question the subsidiary's exercising of power and impose sanctions with varying intensity. For instance, with regard to OECD Guidelines on Multinational Enterprises, the OECD's Investment Committee could issue abstract clarification on the guidelines in instances where National Contact Points did not interpret the guidelines correctly.[169]

164 ILA, *supra* note 156 at 5.

165 *Ibid.*, at 8.

166 *Ibid.*, at 38–39.

167 Wet, *supra* note 157 at 859–860.

168 *Ibid.*, at 866.

169 Gefion Schuler, "Effective Governance through Decentralized Soft Implementation: The OECD Guidelines for Multinational Enterprises" in Armin V. Bogdandy et al., eds,

It is also possible for oversight to be exercised by an independent institution that does not have a hierarchical relationship with the supervised body. In this situation, oversight takes place in a hierarchy because the supervising body acts on the authority of the higher body and reports to it.[170] The Independent Evaluation Group (IEG) at the World Bank exemplifies this type of oversight. The group is institutionally separate from other departments at the Bank and reports directly to the board of executive directors. It rates the Bank's operation programs in accordance with four standards driven from the Bank's own standards: namely, outcome sustainability, institutional impact, and Bank and borrower performance.[171]

Centralized non-judicial complaint procedures, which take place within the institutions themselves, constitute another distinct form of oversight. The most extreme example is that of the Al-Qaeda/Taliban Sanctions Committee's proceedings which allows affected individuals to submit a request for delisting through the United Nations Focal Point.[172] The World Bank also operates the Inspection Panel, which is composed of independent experts and hears complaints from stakeholders adversely affected by the Bank's financed projects.[173]

In sum, in the absence of a national-type mechanism of accountability such as parliamentary oversight or judicial review, general oversight mechanisms could prove helpful in advancing accountability at the supranational level. Current practices of international organizations further illustrate the potential of such mechanisms. At the same time, it is important to realize that the quality of an oversight mechanism depends greatly on the degree to which it shows authority, independence and fairness. The OECD's Investment Committee discussed earlier would barely pass the authority test as it does not have the right to make determinations in regard to specific multinationals, nor reverse the decision of the National Contact Points.[174]

The Exercise of Public Authority by International Institutions: Advancing International Institutional Law (New York: Springer, 2010) 197 at 220–221.

170 Wet, *supra* note 157 at 867.

171 Philipp Dann, "Accountability in Development Aid Law: The World Bank, UNDP and Emerging Structures of Transnational Oversight" (2006) 44 Archiv des Völkerrechts 381 at 392, online: SSRN http://ssrn.com/abstract=1799290; IEG, "About IEG: Improving World Bank Group Development Results through Excellence in Evaluation" (2013) online: IEG http://ieg.worldbankgroup.org/about-us.

172 See the UN Security Council Delisting Procedures, above, for more information.

173 See the World Bank Inspection Panel, above, for more information.

174 In other words, the Investment Committee is precluded from acting as a judicial or quasi-judicial body. It cannot reinvestigate the facts of a specific instance or reach conclusions of its own on the conduct of an enterprise. See, Schuler, *supra* note 169 at 221.

In regard to independence, particular challenges arise from the overlapping of the supervisory body and the supervised body. This is particularly noticeable in the case of the Council for Trade on Services and its subsidiary organ, the Committee on Trade and Financial Services. The fact that the Council for Trade in Services is a plenary body means that the membership of the parent and subsidiary overlaps. This overlapping membership, combined with the technical nature of the Committee's work, makes it unlikely that the Council will conduct a strict review or reach a different conclusion than the Committee. In fact, when reporting to the WTO General Council, the Council for Trade in Services merely refers to the work of the Committee, which is annexed to the report without any further comment.[175]

Finally, the value of an oversight mechanism is greatly affected by the degree of its fairness. Particularly problematic in terms of fairness is the Al-Qaeda/Taliban Sanctions Committee proceedings. While affected individuals can submit a request for delisting through the United Nations Focal Points, they have no right to demand that the Committee consider their requests, nor do they have the right to be heard before the Committee.[176] In contrast, the World Bank Inspection Panel seems to score higher with regard to fairness. The Panel's experts are selected based on their integrity and autonomy from the Bank's management as well as their ability to deal with requests thoroughly and fairly. The proceedings give people and communities, whose interests have

---

175 Joseph Windsor, "The WTO Committee on Trade in Financial Services: The Exercise of Public Authority within an Informational Forum" in V. Bogdandy et al., eds, *The Exercise of Public Authority by International Institutions: Advancing International Institutional Law* (New York: Springer, 2010) 405 at 428–429.

176 Clemens A. Feinäugle, "The UN Security Council Al-Qaida and Taliban Sanctions Committee: Emerging Principles of International Institutional Law for the Protection of Individuals?" in Bogdandy et al., eds, *The Exercise of Public Authority by International Institutions: Advancing International Institutional Law* (New York: Springer, 2010) 101 at 121–122.

As Sarra notes, "at heart, fairness is the capacity to take the perspective of another and to adjust our conduct and decisions to take account of others' perspective in order to achieve more equitable outcomes." When one considers the perspective of those whose liberty and property have been targeted by listing decisions, it seems that they are entitled to have their request heard before the Sanctions Committee. See, Janis Sarra, "Embedding Fairness as a Fundamental Norm in Financial Markets", in Janis Sarra, ed, *An Exploration of Fairness: Interdisciplinary Inquiries in Law, Science and the Humanities* (Carswell: Canada, 2013) 194 at 194.

been affected, greater input into projects sponsored by the Bank and can facilitate redress when warranted.[177]

Conclusion

Legitimacy is a concept whose meaning and sources are often contested. This section was not intended to settle disagreements on this elusive concept in academic literature. Rather, it was an attempt to show that common threads run though different theories and that legitimacy can be nurtured on multiple bases that are not necessarily mutually exclusive. This point seems to particularly be the case with respect to two sources of legitimacy: deliberation and technical performance. Undoubtedly, global banking standards must be set by policy makers who have essential expertise in financial regulation. At the same time, rational discourse with a broader set of stakeholders, such as academics and civil society organizations, can have equally significant benefits. First, such discourse will increase public confidence in the policy making process. Second, it will help policy makers test the assumptions underlying the policies and will make policy makers more successful in detecting systemic risks.

The section drew upon global administrative law (GAL) as a helpful legal theory in assessing the legitimacy of the global governance of banking. I chose to use GAL due to the strengths that I believe it possesses. First, GAL acknowledges that there are significant benefits to international policy making and that collective action is the only way to address issues caused by today's global interdependencies. Second, GAL offers a sound legal understanding of the functions and traits of global governance related to financial regulation. As previously stated, standard setting by transnational regulatory networks shows considerable resemblance to rule making by regulatory agencies, an administrative function distinct from both legislation and adjudication. Third, and most importantly, GAL pays particular attention to procedural safeguards and the contribution they can make to the legitimacy of governance regimes. The GAL sources that were reviewed in this section (domestic administrative law systems as well as current and emerging practices of international institutions) can be used to design appropriate rules and procedures to govern conflict of interest, disclosure, consultation, oversight and redress. However, my project will not draw solely on GAL. As previous discussion suggested, the project will continue to benefit from other theories of political science, jurisprudence and international relations that apply to global financial governance.

177 Word Bank Groups, "The Inspection Panel" (2013) online: World Bank http://web.worldbank.org/WBSITE/EXTERNAL/EXTINSPECTIONPANEL/0,,menuPK:64129249~pagePK:64132081~piPK:64132052~theSitePK:380794,00.html.

After an introduction to the Basel Committee on Banking Supervision as the main research subject, my project will conduct an assessment of the Committee's legitimacy based on the perspectives and criteria identified in this section. The locus of analysis will be the Committee's governance and policy outcomes after the global financial crisis of 2008.The Committee will be considered legitimate to the extent that it meets the requirements of transparency, reasoning and accountability. In regard to accountability, my analysis will be guided by two questions: 1) How and by what means does the BCBS consult the public in its policy making process?; and 2) How and by whom is the Committee's performance monitored? The project will then identify gaps in BCBS legitimacy and will propose policy prescriptions to address those gaps.

I will conclude this section with two general points. First, the legitimacy criteria identified here are not intended to be a set of rigid principles. Indeed, there may be legitimate reasons for trade-offs among these principles, or exceptions to them. For instance, while transparency is an important principle, it should give way to confidentiality when justified by banking regulation necessities. However, one must bear in mind that exceptions must not become so large, either in number or in scope, that they undermine the underlying principle. I will elaborate further on this subject in my project. Second, legitimacy is better considered as a matter of degree. A governance institution, including the BCBS, is not simply legitimate or illegitimate, but rather *more* legitimate or *less* legitimate, depending on how it scores on legitimacy criteria. Institutional change and direction are also factors that need to be taken into account when evaluating legitimacy; an institution whose legitimacy is deteriorating is more questionable than that of an institution that is improving.

Section 3. A Primer on the BCBS History, Governance and Status in the International Financial Architecture

Introduction

The Basel Committee was founded in 1974 at a time when the health of the international financial system was poor and the prospect for international cooperation weak.[178] Financial markets were reeling under the strain of oil price shock and debacles such as the collapse of Bankhaus Herstatt in Germany, which

178 BCBS, "History of the Basel Committee" (Accessed on 25 April 2016) online: BIS http://www.bis.org/bcbs/history.htm [BCBS, "History"].

led to a curb in the foreign exchange markets.[179] The BCBS was initially established to deal with the immediate problems caused by the international financial crises, by providing a forum for education and exchange of information on bank supervision.[180] However, as will be demonstrated below, the Committee's power and influence have gradually grown far beyond its founding mandate.

This section seeks to investigate the BCBS's history and current position in the global regulatory sphere. It aims to establish a general understanding of the BCBS's evolution and current governance and serve as a background for the analyses in subsequent sections. The section starts with an overview of the historical context within which the BCBS was established. It seeks to identify and explain the driving forces behind the establishment of the BCBS, including the rapid expansion of international banking, concerns over the influx of petrodollars into the Eurocurrency markets, the curb in the foreign exchange markets, and collapse of individual banking institutions. The first part also looks at some of the important issues that preoccupied the BCBS founders at the time of its establishment, such as its make-up and function.

The section then turns to key aspects of the BCBS's governance, including membership, mandate, legal position, internal structure and operation, and policy outcomes. In addition to considering important historical factors, the section draws upon new sources of information, such as the recently-adopted *Charter* to explain how the Committee today is organized and conducts its affairs.

The third part takes a step back to consider the BCBS's position in the larger international regulatory regime. It investigates the evolution of the International Financial Architecture (IFA) since the Asian Financial Crisis and attempts to locate the BCBS among the highly-fragmented intuitions that are involved in global financial regulation.

Finally, the section revisits the BCBS as a transnational regulatory network. It draws upon the relevant literature in international relations and international law, to explain the recent rise of the disaggregated state—a phenomenon marking the shift of power from formal international organizations to informal, loosely-structured networks. The paper then proceeds to take a closer look at the networked governance of the BCBS, examining the ways the BCBS has dispensed with traditional formalities associated with formal international organizations.

---

179 Goodhart, *supra* note 19.

180 BCBS, "History", *supra* note 178.

The Historical Context for the BCBS's Establishment

The Emergence of the Eurocurrency Market

As Robert Johnston notes in "The Economics of the Euro-Market: History, Theory and Policy", following the Second World War, the foreign currency business of banks consisted mainly of traditional services such as payments abroad and the financing of national and foreign trade.[181] Sterling continued as an important, if not the main, currency for international trade and London remained the centre for trade finance.[182] With the postwar reconstruction of Europe and large US trade surpluses, the demand for dollar increased and some countries placed restrictions on the import of goods as a means of conserving scarce dollar reserves.[183]

In the late 1950s, two important developments changed the organization of international financial flows. First, following a series of foreign exchange crises between 1955 and 1957, the British authorities restricted the use of sterling in foreign transactions.[184] In particular, use of the sterling to finance non-UK trade was prohibited and the sterling refinancing of trade credits was limited. Second, there was a turnaround in the US's balance of payments. Toward the end of 1950, the US trade surplus gradually vanished. The US government compensated for the decline in surplus by increasing foreign holdings of dollar and capital flows into the US. The abundance of dollar in Europe greatly enhanced its role as the predominant international reserve currency and its use in the financing and invoicing of international trade.[185]

Due to the implemented restriction on sterling use in foreign transactions, British banks began to more actively seek dollar deposits for use in their external obligations.[186] When they were met with a readily available supply of dollar, banks became better positioned to offer customers and correspondent banks dollar facilities instead of sterling credits.[187] By 1958, a European market in dollar deposits and loans was established. There were a number of reasons why investors were inclined to hold their dollar balances in Europe rather than the US. One common view is that some Eastern European banks were afraid that their dollar balances in US might be confiscated due to cold war political

---

181 Robert B. Johnston, *The Economics of the Euro-Market: History, Theory and Policy* (London: McMillan Press, 1983) at 9.

182 *Ibid.*

183 *Ibid.*

184 *Ibid.*

185 *Ibid.*

186 *Ibid.*

187 *Ibid.*

tensions.[188] However, this factor by itself could not have lead to the growth of an active European market in dollar, had it not been for a number of favourable economic and regulatory factors.[189]

The external currency market began to broaden its scope and deepen by the early 1960s, and became known as the Eurodollar, Eurocurrency market and Euromarket. As the market widened, banks from Italy, France, Canada, Japan, Britain, West Germany, as well as foreign branches of US banks, became important participants in the Eurocurrency market. These banks were ready to accept deposits and provide credit in a number of foreign currencies such as pound sterling, Deutsche Mark, and Swiss Francs.[190]

The Rapid Expansion of International Banking

Throughout the 1960s and 1970s, the Eurodollar market continued growing at a remarkable pace. In September 1963—the earliest date for which systemic data of European Banks' foreign currency activities is available—the total short-term foreign currency assets of commercial banks of nine countries reporting to the BIS were $12.4 billion (of which 9.3 billion was in USD).[191] By the end of 1960s, this figure had grown over 500% to 63.4 billion (of which $53 billion was in USD). The 1970s witnessed a structural change in the world's banking system. National banks began establishing a network of subsidiaries and branches aboard to operate in foreign money and Eurocurrency markets.[192]

Brimmer and Dahl document the rapid expansion of foreign branches of US banks in the 1960s–1970s.[193] At the end of 1964, there were only 11 US banks with foreign branches abroad. In combination, these 11 banks operated 181 branches. By the end of 1974, however, there were 129 banks with a total of 737 foreign branches.[194] The total resources of foreign branches of US banks had climbed from $27.1 billion in 1969 to $148.1 billion in 1974.[195]

The growth of the Eurodollar market was significantly driven by national regulations introduced in the 1960s and early 1970s to restrict international capital flows. "These controls shifted the locus of international transactions

188 *Ibid.*

189 *Ibid.*, at 10.

190 *Ibid.*, at 11.

191 *Ibid.*

192 *Ibid.*

193 *Ibid.*

194 Andrew F. Brimmer & Fredrick R. Dahl, "Growth of American International Banking: Implications for Public Policy" (1975) 30:2 *Journal of Finance* 341 at 346.

195 *Ibid.*, at 349.

to the Euro-currency markets and away from national banking systems."[196] A good example of such regulations was the Voluntary Foreign Credit Restraint Program (VFCR), introduced in the US in 1965, which severely limited the ability of US banks to lend directly to foreigners.[197] Under the VFCR, banks in the US were required to keep loans to foreigners and other foreign assets within a certain limit.[198] However, since the program was only applicable to banks located in the US and not their foreign branches, it shifted international finance activities to their foreign branches, which were highly active in the Eurocurrency market.

Another monetary regulation that favoured the development of the Eurocurrency market was Regulation Q.[199] This regulation imposed ceilings on interest rate that banks were permitted to pay on deposits in the US but was not applicable to deposits held by foreign branches. Tight credit conditions in the US and the increase of actual interest rates above Regulation Q ceilings gave banks in the Eurodollar market a competitive advantage in attracting dollar deposits.[200] Johnston notes that the impact of these ceilings on the growth of the Eurodollar market was particularly evident in 1968 and 1969 as interest rates rose during a period of credit restraint. In order to offset large losses of time deposits—which were moving to the banks in the Euromarket that were willing to pay higher interest rates—US banks turned to the Euromarket and their branches abroad as a source of funding. From the end of 1964 to the end of 1969 the Eurodollar claims of European reporting banks on US residents rose from $3 billion to $18 billion.[201]

Corporations in Western Europe used the Eurodollar market as a funding source when domestic credit became tight. In the face of strict monetary controls, West German companies met one-third of their financing needs in 1970 from abroad. UK firms also borrowed heavily in the Eurodollar market during 1960–1970, a period marked by tight domestic credit conditions. Importantly,

196 Johnston, *supra* note 181 at 14.

197 *Ibid.*

198 *Ibid.*

199 Regulation Q. was Title 12, part 217 of the United States Code of Federal Regulations. In 2011, the Federal Reserve Board approved a final rule to repeal the regulation Q. The final rule implemented Section 627 of the *Dodd-Frank Wall Street Reform and Consumer Protection Act*, which repealed Section 19(i) of the *Federal Reserve Act* in its entirety. See for more information, Federal Reserve Board of Governors of the Federal Reserve System, Press Release (14 July 2011) online: Federal Reserve http://www.federalreserve.gov/news-events/press/bcreg/20110714a.htm.

200 Johnston, *supra* note 181 at 14.

201 *Ibid.*

unlike banks in West Germany and the US, banks in the Eurocurrency market were free from holding reserve balances against deposits. Consequently, these banks were able to offer higher interest rates. Short-term interest rates were 0.5 percent higher in the Eurocurrency market than in the US domestic markets.

Increasing Cooperation among Central Banks and the Establishment of the Basel Committee

As suggested above, the Eurocurrency market was developed primarily as a means to escape and exploit domestic controls. It was, therefore, of little surprise that monetary authorities were suspicious of its development. This suspicion was particularly evident in the US where domestic regulations had effectively been neutered by the Eurodollar market, and also in West Germany where the Eurocurrency market made it much harder for the Bundesbank (German central bank) to adhere to the pegged exchange rate and other strict monetary policies.[202]

The world, however, turned upside down with the outbreak of the Arab-Israeli war in October 1973. The war led to a cutback in oil production by the Arab Gulf States and quadruple increase in the price of oil. These events shifted the focus of attention about the Eurodollar market from whether it was exploitative or expansionary to whether it could successfully recycle the petro-dollar from oil exporting countries to oil importers.

This concern garnered greater urgency by the subsequent collapse of the Bankhaus Herstatt in June 1974.[203] Although not a major player, the bank had taken large speculative positions on foreign exchange. When Herstatt became insolvent, the German authorities shut the bank and appointed a receiver. It occurred after the German market was closed but before the closure of the US markets. The receiver insisted that all inward payments to the bank be made but refused to make outward payments until the bankruptcy procedures were completed.[204] Consequently, the banks that had sold Deutsche Mark to Herstatt and expected dollar in return, did not receive anything in return.[205] This badly rattled the foreign exchange market which closed for several days.

The Herstatt debacle was related mainly to the structure of the foreign exchange market and not to the systems of the Euromarket and international capital transfers. The debacle, however, was a reminder of the inherent fragility

202 Goodhart, *supra* note 19 at 29; Brimmer & Dahl, *supra* note 194 at 9–10.

203 Goodhart, *supra* note 19 at 29.

204 *Ibid.*

205 *Ibid.*

of the systems on which the global economy had become heavily reliant.[206] On 3 August 1974, the *Economist* raised the question whether there might be "a world banking crisis?" It articulated three interconnected dimensions of the problem as follows:

> The three big international banking problems of the moment are the dangerous curb in foreign exchange markets, the uncertainty about how oil money will move in the two usual crisis months of August and September, and the way in which fears of crashes are causing money to be withdrawn from small banks all around the world.[207]

Central banks governors then came under significant pressure, particularly from leading politicians, to devise mechanisms and procedures to enhance the stability of the international financial system.[208] However, when the central bank governors met in June 1974 for one of their regular meetings in Basel at the Bank for International Settlements (BIS), vociferous disagreements were expressed around the table.[209] Whereas the US argued that the central banks should make a collective statement expressing their readiness to provide liquidity support to banks operating in the Eurocurrency market, the Germans refused to send such an explicit signal to the markets.[210] They had three important reasons for their refusal. First the Bundesbank did not have a mandate to act as a lender of last resort for foreign banks.[211] Second, the Germans believed that if a bank was in danger of collapse because of managerial incompetence, it should be left to fail. Third, they argued that any blanket assurance would create moral hazard. Thus, the meeting of June 1974 ended without any agreement.[212]

Central banks, were not, however, let off the hook by their domestic banks. Kapstein notes, "as word spread of the disagreement, small banks started to be shut out of the interbank markets, leading them to place strong political pressure on their financial supervisors."[213] Pressured by domestic actors and

206 *Ibid.*, at 32.

207 "A World Banking Crisis", *The Economist* 6832 (3 August 1974) 55 at 55.

208 Ethan B. Kapstein, "Architects of Stability? International Cooperation among Financial Supervisors" (Paper prepared for the Bank for International Settlements 75th Anniversary Conference Basel, Switzerland, June 2005) at 6.

209 *Ibid.*

210 *Ibid.*

211 *Ibid.*

212 *Ibid.*

213 *Ibid.*

politicians, central bank governors returned to Basel for another meeting in September 1974. This time, however, the views seemed to converge and the governors were ready to issue a statement. The press communiqué of the meeting read as follows:

> At their regular meeting in Basel on 9th September, the Central-Bank Governors from the Countries of the Group of Ten and Switzerland discussed the working of the international banking system. They took stock of the existing mechanisms for supervision and regulation and noted recent improvements made in these fields in a major number of countries. They agreed to intensify the exchange of information between central banks on the activities of banks operating in international markets and, where appropriate, to tighten further the regulations governing foreign exchange positions. The governors also had an exchange of views on the problem of the lender of last resort in the Euro-markets. They recognized that it would not be practical to lay down in advance detailed rules and procedures for the provision of temporary liquidity. But they were satisfied that means are available for that purpose and will be used if and when necessary.[214]

The last paragraph of the communiqué attracted much attention from the market participants. Although it was intentionally opaque, there was a signal, for the first time, that the central banks were ready to take on the role of lender of last resort in the Euromarket. Having given this assurance, the central banks were concerned about the inadequate regulation of the Euromarket. Consequently, when returning home, they began to conceptualize the formation of a new G10 subcommittee for bank supervision.[215]

The focus of this new committee was systemic stability, with particular emphasis on the structure and operation of institutions. The nature of its work was to be micro-oriented, particularly in comparison to the *macro*-approach of the existing G10 Eurocurrency Standing Committee.[216] This micro-oriented approach required a different set of expertise than bank supervisors seemed to possess. It should be borne in mind that an authority other than the central bank was in charge of banking supervision in many G10 countries, including Belgium, Canada, Japan, Sweden, Switzerland, and to a degree, France,

---

214 G10 Press Communiqué (September 1974), reprinted in Harold James, *Making the European Monetary Union* (United States: Bank for International Settlement, 2012) at 114.

215 Kapstein, *supra* note 208 at 6.

216 *Ibid.*

Germany, and the US.[217] At the same time, central bank officials were needed on the new committee as they had essential expertise on foreign exchange markets. As previously explained, the Herstatt failure caused massive losses in the foreign exchange markets, indicating that banking crises might well be accompanied with instability in the currency markets. An agreement was therefore made that each country have two representatives on the new committee: one from the prudential authority and one from the central bank.[218] Luxembourg was an exception to this rule, as it did not have a central bank. The new committee was named by the G10 as the Standing Committee on Banking Regulations and Supervisory Practices and George Blunden from the Bank of England was appointed as its first Chairman.[219] The following paragraphs will look in more detail at the governance and operation of this new committee.

BCBS Governance

Designation and Membership

The BCBS did not carry the same name throughout its history. At its inception, it was named the Standing Committee on Banking Regulations and Supervisory Practices. It was however a rather mouthful title, without a catchy acronym. So the Committee came to be known by other shorter names. In early years, the Committee was usually known by the name of its Chairman, first the Blunden Committee (1975–1977) and then the Cooke Committee (1978–1988). It however became a matter of concern to some countries as it would challenge the independence of the Committee or lesson the contribution of countries other than the country of origin of the Chairman. In 1985, the Committee discussed, but took no action on, a note proposing its name be shortened to the Basel Supervisors' Committee. Then in 1989, the BIS Secretariat put forward a note to the Committee proposing alternative names. The Basel Committee on Banking Supervision (BCBS) then emerged as the generally agreed choice.[220]

As previously said, the BCBS was established as a standing committee of the G10. The G10 countries therefore became members as of right. Luxembourg was also granted membership mainly because of its significance as a major Euromarket centre and the influence of Albert Dondelinger, commissiaire au Controle des Banques, in supervisory cooperation among European

217 Goodhart, *supra* note 19 at 4.

218 *Ibid.*, at 41–42.

219 BCBS, "History", *supra* note 178; BCBS, "Chairmen of the Basel Committee" (Accessed on 25 April 2016) online: BIS http://www.bis.org/bcbs/chairmen.htm.

220 Goodhart, *supra* note 19 at 7, Walker, *supra* note 23 at 40–41.

countries.[221] The British argued that membership of the committee should be expanded to include all European Economic Community (EEC) countries, so that all cross-border international issues could be discussed in the forum. The G10 governors were, however, unwilling to dilute committee membership beyond an extra seat for Luxembourg. Thus, Ireland, Denmark, and subsequent entrants to the EU were excluded from the Basel Committee.[222] The limited membership of the BCBS was justified on the basis of the need to facilitate discussion and decision-making, which would be obstructed in a larger grouping. Moreover, 90 percent of the global banking business was then carried on in the G10 jurisdictions and Luxembourg.[223]

At the time, the G10 was the most-established and well-organized international grouping with respect to financial markets. The Group was informally established in 1974 with the support of the IMF, OECD and the BIS by the finance ministers of Belgium, Canada, France, Germany, Italy, Japan, the Netherlands, Sweden, the UK and the US for the primary purpose of intergovernmental discussion regarding the implementation calls upon the lines of credit extended to the IMF. The scope of discussion, however, was broadened over the years. Subsequently, Switzerland became a member of the group, making the 'G10' designation a misnomer. The G10 operated through the finance ministers at the highest level but also through a committee of central bank governors on banking issues. It was the decision of the G10 central bank governors that led to the establishment of the BCBS in 1974.[224]

With the near collapse of the financial systems of major developed economies in 2008–2009, the need to abandon the BCBS exclusive membership to include new economic players became more evident. Thus, following the G20's call in November 2008 to examine participation in standard-setting bodies (SSBs), the BCBS expanded its membership to include Australia, Brazil, China, India, Mexico, South Korea, and Russia.[225] The BCBS was expanded for a second time, following the G20's Summit in London, to include the entire G20

221 Goodhart, *supra* note 19 at 42.

222 *Ibid.*, at 44–45; George Blunden, "Control and Supervision of the Foreign Operations of Banks" in John Edvin Wadsworth et al., eds, *The Development of financial institutions in Europe 1956–1976* (Leyden: Sijthoff, 1977) at 195 [Blunden, "Control and Supervision"].

223 Walker, *supra* note 23 at 44.

224 Joseph J. Norton, "The Work of the Basle Supervisors Committee on Bank Capital Adequacy and the July 1988 Report on 'International Convergence of Capital Measurement and Capital Standards'" (1989) 23 Int'l L. 245 at 248.

225 BCBS, "Expansion of Membership Announced by the Basel Committee" (2009) online: BIS http://www.bis.org/press/p090313.htm.

along with Hong Kong and Singapore.[226] As previously mentioned, representatives on the BCBS come from central banks and prudential authorities and the number of representatives does not normally exceed two, with the exception of the United States, which has four representatives.[227]

A number of regional and international bodies are also observers on the Committee: The European Commission, The European Central Bank, The European Banking Authority, The International Monetary Fund, and The Financial Stability Institute. The BCBS also engages in dialogue with bank supervisors from non-member countries through it subcommittee, the Basel Consultative Group (BCG). The BCG brings together senior representatives from various countries, international institutions and regional groups of banking supervisors that are not members of the Committee.[228]

Legal Position and Mandate

The question of the BCBS's legal position may seem quite simple: the Committee does not have a legal position. Peter Cooke, the BCBS's second Chairman, once said, "the committee does not undertake a formal supranational supervisory role; its conclusions do not have, and were never intended to have, legal force."[229] A similar statement can now be found on the BCBS's own website:

> The Committee's decisions have no legal force. Rather, the Committee formulates supervisory standards and guidelines and recommends statements of best practice in the expectation that individual national authorities will implement them. In this way, the Committee encourages convergence towards common standards and monitors their implementation, but without attempting detailed harmonisation of member countries' supervisory approaches.[230]

---

226 BCBS, "Basel Committee broadens its membership" (2009) online: BIS http://www.bis.org/press/p090610.htm.

227 This is mainly because the US regulatory system is highly fragmented. Representatives come from the Board of Governors of the Federal Reserve System, Federal Reserve Bank of New York, Office of the Comptroller of the Currency, and Federal Deposit Insurance Corporation. See the BCBS, "Basel Committee membership" (Accessed on 25 April 2016) online: BIS http://www.bis.org/bcbs/membership.htm.

228 BCBS, "Main Expert Sub-Committees" (Accessed on 25 April 2016) online: BIS http://www.bis.org/bcbs/mesc.htm [BCBS, "Sub-Committees"].

229 Peter Cooke, "Discussion of the Role of the Committee" (Committee document for external distribution, 21 June 1984), cited in Norton, *supra* note 224 at 249.

230 BCBS, "History", *supra* note 178.

In spite of such disclaimers, the BCBS's policies have important legal implications for national jurisdictions. This issue will be considered in some detail below in discussing the *soft law* characteristics of BCBS's policy outcomes.

As a standing committee of the G10, the BCBS derived its mandate and authority to act from the terms of its appointment.[231] It is important to note that that the BCBS was established as a permanent standing committee. In other words, it was not set up as an *ad hoc* committee to perform a particular task within a fixed time limit. Rather, it was intended to meet periodically throughout the year to discuss the issues of current importance in the field of banking supervision.[232] The G10 governors encouraged the BCBS members to be frank in expressing doubts, criticisms, and raising questions about the adequacy of the supervisory arrangements in countries. It was also the wish of the governors that members solely concern themselves with problems affecting international markets. Matters of purely domestic nature and techniques for dealing with them were not of direct relevance to the Committee.[233]

The BCBS's original objective was relatively modest. Following the decision to set up the Committee, Dr. Zijlstra, then president of the Nederlandsche Bank and the Chairman of the G10, stated that its objective should not be to make far-fetched attempts to harmonize supervisory systems in member countries. Rather, it would attempt "to enable its members to learn from each other and to apply the knowledge so acquired to improving their own systems of supervision, so indirectly enhancing the likelihood of overall stability in the international banking system".[234] While issues of liquidity support were to be considered by the G10 central bank governors, regulatory and supervisory issues were to be considered by the new standing committee.[235]

A striking change in the BCBS's activity, however, started with the capital adequacy harmonization in the second half of the 1980s. The extension of the BCBS's activities to substantive supervisory rules was mainly prompted by the pressure exerted by some BCBS members concerned about the declining capitalization of their banks and the risk of a race to bottom in prudential supervision. US authorities in particular were deeply concerned about the sound capitalization of American banking intermediaries in the wake of

231 Walker, *supra* note 23 at 51.

232 *Ibid.*; Blunden, "Control and Supervision", *supra* note 222 at 195.

233 George Blunden, "Opening Remarks Draft for the BCBS First Meeting" (24 January 1974), cited in Goodhart, *supra* note 19 at 45–47 [Blunden, "Opening Remarks"].

234 Blunden, "Control and Supervision", *supra* note 222 at 195.

235 Walker, *supra* note 23 at 51.

the 1980s debt crisis.[236] A move towards greater capital ratios could endanger the competiveness of US banks, particularly in contrast to the Japanese banks.[237] As a result, the first Capital Accord was based on two important considerations. First, the framework would "serve to strengthen the soundness and stability of the international banking system". Second, it was intended to be "fair and consistent in its application to international banks in different countries so as to diminish one important source of competitive inequality".[238] The harmonization of capital standards stands in sharp contrast to the low-key collaboration that distinguished the BCBS's earlier policy initiatives, such as the 1975 Concordat.[239] Whereas the Concordat merely endorsed the generally accepted principles that guide coordination among home and host authorities, Basel I dealt specifically with capital adequacy rules.[240] Such rules were then significantly expanded in scope and detail by subsequent amendments, including Basel II and Basel III.

The BCBS's current mandate is set out in its new *Charter*, which was endorsed in January 2013 by the Group of Governors and Heads of Supervision (GHOS), the BCBS's oversight body. The first thing to note about the *Charter* is that it does not change the formal position of the BCBS.[241] Neither the *Charter* nor the Committee has formal legal status under international law. The *Charter* sets the BCBS's objectives and operating modalities and is intended to enhance understanding of the Committee's activities and decision-making processes.[242] It considers the BCBS "the primary global standard-setter for the prudential regulation of banks", and "a forum for cooperation on banking supervisory matters."[243] The BCBS's mandate is to strengthen the regulation, supervision and practices of banks worldwide with the purpose of enhancing

236 Wood, *supra* note 31 at 70–72.

237 *Ibid.*, at 75.

238 BCBS, "Outcome of the Consultative Process on Proposals for International Convergence of Capital Measurement and Capital Standards" (July 1988) at para 3, online: BIS http://www.bis.org/publ/bcbs04b.pdf.

239 BCBS, *Report on the Supervision of Banks' Foreign Establishments—Concordat* (September 1975) online: BIS http://www.bis.org/publ/bcbs00a.htm; Enrico L. Camilli, "Basel–Brussels One Way? The EU in the Legalization Process of Basel Soft Law" in Edoardo Chiti & Bernardo G. Mattarella, eds, *Global Administrative Law and EU Administrative Law: Relationships, Legal Issues and Comparison* (Berlin: Springer, 2011) 324 at 334–335.

240 *Ibid.*

241 BCBS, "Group of Governors and Heads of Supervision Endorses Revised Liquidity Standard for Banks" (2013) online: BIS http://www.bis.org/press/p130106.htm.

242 *Ibid.*

243 *Charter, supra* note 38, s 1.

financial stability."[244] Such a mandate is achieved through an array of activities, including: exchange of information on recent developments in the banking sector and financial markets; sharing supervisory issues and techniques to promote common understanding and cross-border cooperation; establishing and promoting standards, guidelines, and sound practices for bank regulation; addressing gaps that pose threats to financial stability; monitoring the implementation of the BCBS's standards; consulting with central banks and supervisory authorities of non-member countries; and coordination and cooperation with other financial sector standard-setters and international bodies.[245]

Thus, the BCBS's mandate is now considerably broader than its original purpose, namely providing a medium for education and exchange of information about bank supervision. As indicated by its *Charter*, the BCBS is "the primary global standard-setter for the prudential regulation of banks". In fact, the BCBS's post-crisis mandate goes beyond setting standards to include the surveillance of their implementation in member countries and beyond. This issue will be considered in more detail in subsequent sections.

Internal Structure and Operation

Historically, the nature and operation of the BCBS have been noted for their legal and procedural informality. Due to the highly secretive nature of its operation, a large amount of uncertainty has always surrounded the Committee's operation. Once the decision was made by the G10 to establish the new standing committee in December 1974, no separate directions were provided with respect to the structure and method of its operation.[246] The early operations of the Committee were left to its first Chairman, George Blunden. In an interview with George Walker, Blunden said that he had to arrange a number of meetings with the Committee's first secretary, Michael Daltry to discuss various preparatory issues prior to the first meeting in February 1975.[247] The focus of such meetings was, however, what was to be achieved by the Committee rather than operational or structural issues. As a result, the nature and character of the BCBS's meetings and operations were developed naturally, or perhaps accidentally, over time.[248]

Although still nominally informal, the Committee now seems to operate in a carefully structured and organized manner, which is consistent with its

244 *Charter, ibid.*, s 1.

245 *Charter, ibid.*, s 2.

246 Walker, *supra* note 23 at 39.

247 *Ibid.*

248 *Ibid.*, at 40.

growing stature and its extended mandate. The most up-to-date source of information on the current organizational structure and operation of the BCBS is its *Charter*. Under s. 7, the BCBS's internal structure comprises four bodies: 1) the Committee; 2) Groups, Working Groups and Task Forces; 3) the Chairman; and 4) the Secretariat.[249]

The Committee is the ultimate decision-making body of the BCBS, ensuring that the BCBS's mandate is achieved.[250] It normally meets four times per year but the Chairman can hold additional meetings, if necessary.[251] There has never been a formal voting system within the BCBS and all decisions are decided by consensus.[252]

BCBS members and observers are entitled to appoint one representative to attend the "committee" meetings. These representatives should be senior officials of their institutions such as head of banking supervision, head of banking policy/regulation, central bank deputy governor, head of financial stability department or the equivalent. More importantly, the representatives should have the authority to commit their institutions.[253]

The main responsibilities of the Committee include: developing and monitoring the BCBS's work program with general guidance provided by the GHOS; establishing and promoting the BCBS's standards, guidelines and best practices; establishing and disbanding groups, working groups and task forces; deciding on organizational regulations governing its activities; recommending amendments to the BCBS's *Charter* to the GHOS.[254]

The Committee's work is organized around Groups, Working Groups, and Task Forces.[255] Groups are subcommittees that report directly to the Committee. They are composed of senior staff who undertake major areas of the Committee's work.[256] At present, the BCBS has five major Groups:

1. The Supervision and Implementation Group (SIG) serves two primary objectives: fostering timely, consistent, and effective implementation of the Basel Committee's standards and guidelines; and advancing improvements in banking supervision, particularly in member countries. That SIG

249 *Charter, supra* note 38, s 7.
250 *Charter, ibid.*, s 8.
251 *Charter, ibid.*, s 8.2.
252 *Charter, ibid.*, s 8.4; Goodhart, *supra* note 19 at 547.
253 *Charter, ibid.*, s 8.4.
254 *Charter, ibid.*, s 8.1.
255 *Charter, ibid.*, s 9.
256 *Charter, ibid.*, s 9.1.

has a number of Working Groups and Task Forces that work on specific issues such as the *Working Group on Operational Risk, Working Group on Supervisory Colleges*, and *Working Group on Systemically Important Banks Supervision*.[257]

2. The Policy Development Group (PDG) assists the Committee by developing policies which promote a sound banking system and high supervisory standards. The PDG special Working Groups include *Woking Group on Capital, Trading Book Working Group, Securitisation Working Group, Working Group on Liquidity*, and *Working Group on Disclosure*.
3. The Macroprudential Supervision Group (MPG) monitors and reports to the Committee on systemic risk and developments related to the macroprudential oversight and systemically important banks (SIB). It also provides guidance to the work of other groups and develops policy proposals which may be needed to address gaps and inconsistencies in the overall framework of macroprudential/SIB supervision.[258]
4. The Accounting Experts Group (AEG) works to ensure that international accounting and auditing standards promote sound risk management, market discipline, and safety and soundness of the banking system. It provides guidance on prudential reporting and takes an active role in the development of accounting and auditing standards.
5. The BCG, which as mentioned earlier, provides a forum to facilitate the Committee's engagement with supervisors around the world. In particular, it fosters dialogue between the Committee and prudential authorities of non-member jurisdictions.[259]

The Chairman is appointed by the GHOS for a term of three years, which can be renewed once.[260] The Chairman convenes and chairs meetings and directs the work of the Committee in accordance with its mandate.[261] In addition, the Chairman represents the BCBS externally and is the main spokesperson for the BCBS.[262]

The BCBS Secretariat is provided by the BIS. The secretariat is primarily comprised of professional staff who are usually on temporary secondment from

257 BCBS, "Sub-Committees", *supra* note 228.

258 *Ibid.*

259 *Ibid.*

260 *Charter, supra* note 38, s 10.1.

261 *Charter, ibid.*, ss 10, 10.2.

262 *Charter, ibid.*, s 10.2.

BCBS members.[263] Some of the important responsibilities of the Secretariat are: providing support and assistance to the Committee, Chairman, and Groups; ensuring timely and effective flow of information to the BCBS members and facilitating contact between the BCBS members and non-members; and maintaining and administering the BCBS records and website.[264]

The GHOS is the oversight body of the BCBS. The BCBS reports to the GHOS and seeks its endorsement for its major decisions. In addition the GHOS has the responsibility for approving amendments to the BCBS *Charter*, proving general directions for the BCBS's work program and appointing the BCBS's Chairman from among its members.[265]

Policy Outcomes

The BCBS's policy outcomes can be considered under three main categories. The first category is the *standards* for prudential regulation and supervision of banks.[266] These standards primarily apply to internationally active banks, although they might be applied more broadly. It is important to remember that the BCBS's standards constitute the *minimum* prudential requirements. Countries may, therefore, decide to go beyond them.[267] The second group of policies are *guidelines*, designed to elaborate upon and provide additional guidance for implementation of standards.[268] The Committee has also issued guidance for a wider range of issues including corporate governance, liquidity risk management, operational risk, stress testing, and supervisory colleges.[269] Finally, the BCBS issues sound practices. These documents describe actual observed practices, with the goal of promoting common understanding

263 *Charter, ibid.*, s 11.

264 *Charter, ibid.*, s 11.1.

265 *Charter, ibid.*, s 6.

266 *Charter, ibid.*, s 12.

267 For examples of standards see, BCBS, "Core Principles for Effective Banking Supervision" (2012) http://www.bis.org/publ/bcbs230.htm; BCBS, "Liquidity Coverage Ratio Disclosure Standards—Consultative Document" (2013) online: BIS http://www.bis.org/publ/bcbs259.htm; BCBS, "Capital Requirements for Bank Exposures to Central Counterparties" (2012) online: BIS http://www.bis.org/publ/bcbs227.htm.

268 *Charter, supra* note 38, s 13.

269 For examples of guidelines, see BCBS, "Guidance for National Authorities Operating the Countercyclical Capital Buffer" (2010) online: BIS http://www.bis.org/publ/bcbs187.htm; BCBS, "Operational Risk—Supervisory Guidelines for the Advanced Measurement Approaches—Final Document" (2011) online: BIS http://www.bis.org/publ/bcbs196.htm; BCBS, "Supervisory Guidance for Managing Risks Associated with the Settlement of Foreign Exchange Transactions" (2013) online: BIS http://www.bis.org/publ/bcbs241.htm.

and improving supervisory and banking practices.[270] Members and banks are encouraged to compare these practices with those applied in their own jurisdictions so that they may identify areas for improvement. Stress testing, asset securitization, resolution and remuneration are among the recent themes of sound practices.[271]

The most important policy outcomes of the BCBS—which will be also the focus of this project—are standards. While the BCBS members are *encouraged to adopt best practices*, they are *expected to implement standards* in full.[272] The key standards are capital and liquidity requirements for internationally active banks. These requirements are set in the Basel Accords, which have been revised at different stages. The most recent Accord is Basel III, which includes the reforms adopted after the GFC.

The BCBS's policy outcomes, particularly the standards, are considered *soft law*. Soft law refers to rules that are not legally binding but in practice are adhered to by those addressed or by others for various reasons such as moral suasion or fear of adverse action.[273] The term *soft law* is usually used in contrast to *hard law*. While hard law is characterized by formality, soft law is characterized by informality. Moreover, hard law is binding in a coercive and externally-imposed fashion, but soft law is obeyed in a voluntary and self-imposed manner. Enforcement is, therefore, the key distinction between soft law and hard law. As Giovanoli puts it, "from the legal point of view, no remedies are available if the rules are not followed. This does not, of course, preclude the existence of factual sanctions, either from the market or from other bodies, which can be very effective."[274]

The soft-law nature of BCBS's decisions can help with understanding why the Basel Capital Accords have been widely implemented. Basel I was recognized as one of the most successful international regulatory initiatives. In

---

270 *Charter, supra* note 38, s 14.

271 See, e.g., BCBS, "Report and Recommendations of the Cross-border Bank Resolution Group—Final Paper" (2010) online: BIS http://www.bis.org/publ/bcbs169.htm; BCBS, "Sound Practices for Backtesting Counterparty Credit Risk Models—Final Document" (2010) online: BIS http://www.bis.org/publ/bcbs185.htm; BCBS, "Principles for Enhancing Corporate Governance—Final Document" (2010) online: BIS: http://www.bis.org/publ/bcbs176.htm; BCBS, "Good Practice Principles on Supervisory Colleges—Final Document" (2010) online: BIS http://www.bis.org/publ/bcbs177.htm.

272 *Charter, supra* note 38, s 5(e).

273 Roy Goode, *Commercial Law*, 2d ed (London: Penguin, 1995) at 20–21.

274 Mario Giovanoli, "A New Architecture for the Global Financial Market: Legal Aspects of International Financial Standard Setting" in Mario Giovanoli, ed, *International Monetary Law, Issues for the New Millennium* (Oxford: Oxford University Press, 2000) 3 at 35.

addition to its promulgation by the BCBS members, more than 100 countries implemented the accord in their national systems.[275] The implementation of Basel II was associated with a number of complications that will be considered at some length in the last section. Here it suffices to note that Basel II came into force in 2006 and by 2008, when the globe was fully emerged in a financial crisis, 57 countries were in the process of implementing all or parts of the Basel II framework.[276] Finally, with respect to Basel III, which came into force in January 2013, 25 BCBS members (out of 27) issued the final rules by August 2013.[277] The remaining two member jurisdictions have issued draft rules.[278]

Since the early days of the BCBS, its members had established the unwritten rule that once the proposals were agreed upon within the committee and endorsed by the governors, members were honor-bound to implement them.[279] Non-member countries also had important incentives to comply with BCBS's policies. If they did not implement the standards, the BCBS members might deny them access to their financial markets. Additionally, the Financial Sector Assessment Program (FSAP), a joint IMF-World Bank surveillance initiative, introduced in 1999, indirectly enforced the BCBS's standards.[280] An important component of the FSAP was Reports on Observance of Standards and Codes (ROSCs), which summarised the extent to which countries observed internationally recognized standards, including those adopted by the BCBS.[281] These evaluations, therefore, provided the non-G10 countries with an important incentive to observe the BCBS's standards.[282] The FSAP will be discussed in greater detail under the next heading.

With the backing of the G20, the BCBS has recently established a more active program to monitor the implementation of its standards, particularly Basel III, including through publishing periodic reports on the progress made in implementation of standards, and producing detailed assessments of national

275 Anupam Prakash, "Evolution of the Basel Framework on Bank Capital Regulation" (Reserve Bank of India Occasional Papers Vol. 29, No. 2, Monsoon, 2008) at 85.

276 *Ibid.*, at 102.

277 BCBS, "Report to G20 Leaders on Monitoring Implementation of Basel III Regulatory Reforms" (August 2013) at 3, online: BIS http://www.bis.org/publ/bcbs260.pdf.

278 *Ibid.*

279 Goodhart, *supra* note 19 at 554–555.

280 IMF, "Financial Sector Assessment Program (FSAP)" (10 June 2014) online: IMF http://www.imf.org/external/NP/fsap/fssa.aspx.

281 World Bank, "RSOC—Reports on Observance of Standards and Codes" (Accessed on 25 April 2016) online: World Bank http://www.worldbank.org/ifa/rosc_more.html.

282 Goodhart, *supra* note 19 at 554–555.

regulations against the agreed international standards.[283] The BCBS surveillance program will be considered in more detail in the next section.

The BCBS and the International Financial Architecture

The International Financial Architecture (IFA) includes various institutions that produce international financial standards (IFS). Broadly speaking, the IFS refers to a wide range of principles, practices and guidelines that establish the rules of the game in the global financial markets and provide the framework within which financial institutions operate and financial policies are devised and implemented.[284] The development of IFS started in earnest after the Asian Financial Crisis (AFC).[285] Following the crisis, Robert Rubin, the Secretary of the United States Treasury gave a lecture at the Brookings Institution, stressing the need to strengthen the *International Financial Architecture*. This was the first time the term IFA was used and the lecture was considered to open a new chapter in the regulation of international finance.[286]

It was then understood that the Asian Financial Crisis happened largely due to inadequate regulation and supervision of financial institutions, particularly in crisis-stricken countries. There was therefore a strong need to upgrade the regulatory frameworks to the requirements of global finance and to safeguard the stability of the international system against future crisis.[287]

International financial institutions in Washington, particularly the IMF, then started to push for "sequencing project", meaning that before liberalizing their capital accounts, countries should upgrade their regulatory regime.[288] Washington institutions called for greater transparency and a set of detailed standards to ensure financial safety and to reduce the excessive risk of financial integration. Standard-setting bodies such as the BCBS, Financial Stability Forum (which was subsequently re-founded as the Financial Stability Board), International Organization of Securities Commissions (IOSCO) and International Accounting Standards Board (ISAB), were assigned to develop

283 BCBS, "The Basel Committee's Work" (Accessed on 25 April 2016) online: BIS http://www.bis.org/bcbs/bcbs_work.htm.

284 Mario Giovanoli, "The Reform of the International Financial Architecture after the Global Crisis" (2009) 42 *International Law and Politics* 81 at 84 [Giovanoli, "Reform of the IFA"].

285 Peter B. Kenen, *The International Financial Architecture: What's New? What's Missing?* (Washington: Institute for International Economics, 2001) at 1.

286 *Ibid.*

287 *Ibid.*, at 10; Jakob Vestergard, *Discipline in Global Economy: International Finance and End of Liberalism* (New York: Routledge, 2009) at 123.

288 IMF, "Financial Sector Assessment: A Handbook" (29 September 2005) at 317–320, online: IMF http://www.imf.org/external/pubs/ft/fsa/eng/.

standards and codes of best practices.[289] These standards covered 12 areas that could be grouped under three main categories:

1. **Policy transparency**, including data transparency, fiscal transparency, monetary and fiscal policy transparency;
2. **Financial Sector Regulation and Supervision**, including standards in the areas of banking, securities, insurance, payment systems and anti-money laundering and combating the financing of terrorism; and
3. **Market integrity**, including three areas of corporate governance, accounting, auditing and insolvency and credit rights.[290]

The coordination of these efforts was assigned to the IMF and the World Bank. The IMF primarily coordinated the efforts in the first two areas (policy transparency and Financial Sector Regulation and Supervision), while the World Bank held responsibility for the third area of standards.

The system of standards went hand in hand with a system of surveillance. In their declaration on 3 October 1998, the G7 called upon all countries "to comply with internationally agreed codes and standards". More importantly, they asked the IMF "to monitor the implementation of these codes and standards" and "to publish in a timely and systematic way the results of its surveillance of the degree to which each of its member countries" was successful in compliance with the standards.[291] The surveillance that was established for this purpose was the Financial Sector Assessment Program (FSAP), which will be considered in more detail later.

In spite of their scope and sophistication, IFS were unable to prevent or mitigate the GFC. Some key standards played an enabling role in the crisis, contributing to the emergence, aggravation and dissemination of the crisis.[292] Consequently, it became evident that both the IFA and the IFS had to be reformed. The political support for these reform initiatives was provided by the G20, an informal forum that "promotes open and constructive discussion between industrial and emerging-market countries on key issues related

---

289 G7, "Declaration of G7 Finance Ministers and Central Bank Governors" (30 October 1998) online: IMF http://www.imf.org/external/np/g7/103098dc.htm.

290 FSB, "Compendium of Standards" (Accessed on 25 April 2016) online: FSB http://www.fsb.org/what-we-do/about-the-compendium-of-standards/

291 G7, *supra* note 289.

292 Giovanoli, "Reform of the IFA", *supra* note 284 at 87.

to global economic stability".[293] G20 was more or less inactive since its inception in 1999 until 2008 when it was revived as the main forum for reforming international financial architecture.[294] To prevent future crises, G20 leaders committed to repairing the financial system, strengthening financial supervision and regulation, and reforming global financial institutions.[295] International standard-setting bodies (SSBs) were required to reform their existing standards and develop new ones. The Financial Stability Forum was reinvented as the Financial Stability Board (FSB) to coordinate the activities of the SSBs and to develop and promote the implementation of effective regulatory and supervisory policies.[296]

The new international financial architecture bears significant resemblance to the old regime. It consists of highly fragmented institutions that perform three sets of activities related to international financial regulation: setting agendas, developing standards, and monitoring compliance. The first activity is mainly associated with the G20, and in particular its technocratic extension, the FSB. These bodies operate at the core of the IFA, determining the objectives that need to be achieved and issues that need to be addressed through regulation. Some of the recent agenda includes strengthening macroprudential oversight,[297] improving the transparency and regulation of over-the-counter (OTC) derivatives,[298] and intensifying regulation and supervision of Systemically Important Financial Institutions (SIFIs).[299] The second activity, namely devising guidance for market participants, is largely undertaken by the SSBs, which set standards for various financial sectors. The categorization and

---

293 Global Partnership for Financial Inclusion, "About the G20" online: Global Partnership for Financial Inclusion http://gpfi.org/about-gpfi/about-the-g20.

294 Giovanoli, "Reform of the IFA", *supra* note 284 at 90.

295 G20, "Global Plan for Recovery and Reform" (April 2009) online: G20 Information Centre http://www.g20.utoronto.ca/2009/2009communique0402.html.

296 G20, "Declaration on Strengthening the Financial System", (April 2009) online: G20 Information Centre http://www.g20.utoronto.ca/2009/2009ifi.pdf.

297 See, e.g., FSB, "Macroprudential Policy Tools and Frameworks—Update to G20 Finance Ministers and Central Bank Governors" (February 2011) online: FSB http://www.financialstabilityboard.org/list/fsb_pa/tid_161/index.htm; FSB, "Addressing Financial System Procyclicality: A Possible Framework" (April 2009) online: FSB http://www.financialstabilityboard.org/publications/r_0904e.htm.

298 See, e.g., FSB, "Implementing OTC Derivatives Market Reforms" (October 2010) online: FSB http://www.financialstabilityboard.org/list/fsb_pa/tid_172/index.htm.

299 See, e.g., FSB, Policy Measures to Address Systemically Important Financial Institutions (November 2011) online: FSB http://www.financialstabilityboard.org/publications/r_111104bb.pdf.

areas of standards remains the same as the previous regime, outlined above [under section … OR on page …]. Finally, monitoring takes place in different forms including peer reviews. However, the IMF and the World Bank still retain their surveillance function through the FSAP.

The BCBS's mandate and policy outcomes, as discussed above, suggest that it primarily fits with the second category, namely, SSBs. In fact, the Committee is the oldest financial standard-setter, with 8 percent capital requirement for banks, widely known as the prime example of the IFS. However, the technical nature of the Committee's work and its stature gives it significant leeway in setting its own agenda. In addition, the introduction of the surveillance program for banking standards implies that the Committee has taken on a monitoring role. Thus, the BCBS's current functions seem to overlap with all three categories of activities in international financial regulation.

The Committee maintains channels for coordination with supervisors of non-bank financial institutions, a prime example being the Joint Forum (whose role as an important consultation base will be considered more fully later). Here, it suffices to say that the Joint Forum was established in 1996 under the aegis of the Basel Committee, IOSCO, and the International Association of Insurance Supervisors (IAIS) to address issues common to banking, securities, and insurance. The BCBS has also worked on a number of technical banking and auditing issues with other specialized SSBs such as the International Financial Reporting Standards Foundation (IFRS Foundation), the International Federation of Accountants (IFAC), and the International Forum of Independent Audit Regulators (IFIAR). This work has resulted in papers on topics such as the relationship between bank supervisors and external auditors and uniform rules for foreign exchange contracts.[300]

Revisiting the BCBS as a Transnational Regulatory Network

Up until the present, international financial regulation and supervision have largely been conducted by institutions that rely on *soft* administrative structures. These institutions are not set up by international law instruments but rather by bylaws, agreements, and declarations that have no formal sense of international obligation or existence. On the other hand, formal international organizations mostly play a supporting role in financial regulation. They help monitor implementation of standards and provide administrative support for

300 BCBS, "Basel Committee Cooperation with Other Standard-setting Bodies" (Accessed on 25 April 2016) online: BIS www.bis.org/bcbs/coop_with_sec_and_ins.htm.

regulatory bodies that do not have secretariats. International organizations are, however, rarely a direct source of international financial regulation.[301]

Recent decades have witnessed a tendency on the part of states and sub-state entities to search for alternative methods of cooperation and rule-making that are less formal and institutionalized. Anne-Marie Slaughter argues that this trend indicates the emergence of a new world order, shifting the locus of power from traditional organizations to transgovernmental networks.[302] She defines *network* as "a pattern of regular and purposive relations among like government units working across the borders that divide countries and demarcate the 'domestic' from the 'international' sphere."[303] Networks "allow domestic officials to interact with their foreign counterparts directly, without much supervision by foreign offices or senior executive branch officials".[304] They demonstrate "loosely structured, peer-to-peer ties developed through frequent interaction rather than formal negotiation".[305]

The rise of networks is characterized as a corollary of the rise of *disaggregated state*. Whereas countries were traditionally represented on the international scene by heads of state or foreign ministries, powers have increasingly been delegated to sub-state administrative agencies and regulators. These regulators or agencies have to address cross-border questions that lay within their regulatory mandate. Under traditional international law, the new actors cannot normally represent the state unless they are specifically accredited to do so. Thus, instead of resorting to formal international organizations and formal law making, these actors use networks and informal law making.[306]

Traditional explanations for the rise of networks often focus on procedural efficiency. By adopting informal rules of organization, participants retain flexibility to establish, reform, and dissolve institutions quickly. For instance, financial regulators do not require governmental consent to participate in international organizations or to assemble a multilateral treaty conference for developing financial standards. Instead, in collaboration with their colleagues, regulators organize an informal network to collaborate on international

---

301 Brummer, *supra* note 80 at 63–64.

302 Anne-Marie Slaughter, *A New World Order* (Princeton, NJ: Princeton University Press, 2004) at 14.

303 *Ibid.*

304 *Ibid.*

305 Anne-Marrie Slaughter & David Zaring, "Networks Go International: An Update" (2006) 6:12 *Annual Review of Law and Social Science* 215 at 215.

306 Joost Pauwelyn, Ramses A. Wessel & Jan Wouters, "The Exercise of Public Authority through Informal International Lawmaking: An Accountability Issue?" (Jean Monnet Working Paper 06/11, New York University School of Law, 2011) at 13.

problems.[307] In addition, reforming networks seems easier in comparison to formal international organizations where enlargement or reform of membership may require renegotiation of treaties and ratification by national legislatures.[308] Speed, adaptability, and effectiveness in addressing new and unexpected challenges are also important reasons that explain the proliferation of transgovernmental networks.

The BCBS's governance and method of operation, as discussed above, clearly indicates that it is a transgovernmental regulatory network. A close examination reveals that the BCBS has dispensed with certain formalities traditionally linked to international law. These formalities are closely associated with *actors, process* and *outputs*, which will be discussed in turn below.[309]

First, in terms of *actor*, the BCBS's operation is informal in the sense that it does not engage traditional diplomatic actors, such as heads of states or foreign ministers. Under article 7 of the Vienna Convention on the Law of Treaties, only heads of state, foreign ministers, heads of diplomatic missions or specifically accredited representatives are presumed to have so-called full power to represent or bind a state.[310] The Basel Committee, however, is solely composed of officials from central banks and supervisory authorities.[311] These officials are not diplomats who represent their states, but bureaucrats representing sub-state agencies.

As Slaughter notes, "the essence of a network is a process rather than an entity; thus it cannot be captured or controlled in the ways that typically structure formal legitimacy in a democratic polity".[312] The *process* of international cooperation in BCBS is informal in the sense that it occurs in a loosely organized forum rather than a formal international organization. Unlike WTO or UN, the BCBS has little physical presence; it does not have its own budget, permanent staff or headquarters. Instead it operates under the auspices of the BIS. BCBS meetings and decision-making are considerably less tightly-regulated in comparison to international organizations. It must also be acknowledged that

307 David Zaring, "Informal Procedure, Hard and Soft, in International Administration" (2005) 5:2 Chi J Int'l L 547 at 578.

308 Brummer, *supra* note 80 at 64.

309 For a more detailed discussion of the characteristics of actors, processes and outcomes involved in informal international law making, see Pauwelyn, Wessel & Wouters, *supra* note 306 at 8–13.

310 *Vienna Convention on the Law of Treaties*, 23 May 1969, UNTS 18232, art. 7.

311 *Charter, supra* note 38, s 4.

312 Anne-Marie Slaughter, "Agencies on the Loose? Holding Government Networks Accountable" (Public Law and Legal Theory Working Paper No. 006, 1999) at 10, online: SSRN http://papers.ssrn.com/sol3/papers.cfm?abstract_id=209319.

the Committee was informally constituted. It was not founded by an international treaty but by a press communiqué issued by the G10 governors. As a consequence of this informal process, the BCBS is less constrained by the controls under domestic or international law. Bank supervisors within the BCBS face fewer constraints than in their purely domestic capacities or as formal delegates to international organizations.

Finally, the BCBS's *outputs* are informal in the sense that they do not lead to formal treaties or any other traditional source of international law, but rather to standards, guidelines and sound practices. At the domestic level, this output informality leads to weaker forms of oversight. For instance, in the US, Circular 175 procedure of the State department is designed to ensure the proper exercise of treaty making power and prescribes requirements for publication and transmittal of international agreements to the US Congress. This Circular, however, does not apply to the BCBS's documents because they "are not binding under international law".[313] The US constitutional rule that a two-third majority in the Senate must adopt treaties also does not apply to international agreements, which are not classified as treaties.[314] Similarly, in the UK, the formalities surrounding treaty-making does not include memoranda of understandings, which refers to those international commitments not legally binding.[315]

Conclusion

The BCBS was established at a time when existing institutional mechanisms were inadequate to cope with the risks arising from the international operations of financial intermediaries. Its establishment was an example of a larger trend to give authority to technical experts to deal with complex social and economic problems. The BCBS was founded as a transnational network intended to minimize the hardship of, and costs involved with, establishing formal international organizations. Its establishment represents a tradeoff in favour of informal constitution, minimal institutionalization, and closed operation.

The BCBS's network governance implies less representative legitimacy in contrast to formal international organizations, which are rooted in international law. Arguably, however, the BCBS's network attributes can nurture

313 US Department of State, "Circular 175 Procedure" (Accessed on 25 April 2016) online: Bureau of Public Affairs http://www.state.gov/s/l/treaty/c175/.

314 Pauwelyn, Wessel & Wouters, *supra* note 306 at 20.

315 Foreign & Commonwealth Office, "Treaties and MOUS: Guidance on Practice and Procedures" (March 2013) at 1, online: Government Digital Service: https://www.gov.uk/government/publications/treaties-and-mous-guidance-on-practice-and-procedures.

other foundations for its legitimacy. The BCBS's expertise and relative insulation from political interference indicates a higher likelihood of delivering public goods, particularly greater financial stability. Moreover, strong peer-to-peer ties among bank supervisors, twinned with institutional flexibility and consensus-based decisionmaking can be viewed as enhancing the deliberative quality of the BCBS's policy making.

Nevertheless, two caveats with respect to the argument that the BCBS's networked governance enhance its legitimacy need to be voiced here. First, the global financial crisis of 2008 came to discredit international financial standards, including the prudential standards adopted by the BCBS. Such failure casts a shadow on the BCBS's outcome-based legitimacy, reviving the public choice theorists' concern that specialized technocratic bodies are prone to capture by private interests. The BCBS's deliberative-based legitimacy also seems constrained, given that the Committee is solely comprised of officials from central banks and supervisory authorises—in other words, like-minded individuals with similar education and career backgrounds. Without mechanisms that provide exposure to competing views and access to a larger pool of arguments, the BCBS is in danger of adopting inferior policies.

Since the onset of the GFC, the BCBS has taken some modest steps towards greater formalization, such as the adoption of the BCBS *Charter* and surveillance of the implementation of banking standards. Such steps, however, have been adopted with the political backing of the G20, which itself remains an informal and loose forum for international cooperation. While the BCBS *Charter* and the surveillance of post-crisis reforms reflect a greater realization of the need for international cooperation and robust implementation of agreed reforms, they have not yet changed the underlying network characteristics of the BCBS. It remains to be seen whether such steps will ultimately give rise to a shift in the locus power from networks back to more formal and institutionalized regimes of governance.

List of References

Legislation

Administrative Procedure Act (Verwaltungsverfahrensgesetz, VwVfG), 25 May 1976, Federal Law Gazette I p. 102 (Germany).

Dodd-Frank Wall Street Reform and Consumer Protection Act, Pub. L. No.111–203, § 619, 24 Stat. 1376 (2010).

General Administrative Law Code (Algemene wet bestuursecht, AWB), June 1992, Official Journal (Staatsblad) 1994, nr. A (Netherlands).

Administrative Procedure Act, 5 USC § 553(c) (2000).

Administrative Procedure Act, 7 August 1990, Law N. 241, (Italy).

Jurisprudence

Marbury v Madison, 1 Cranch 137, 2 L Ed 60 (1803) (US).

Conseild'Etat, 19 Feb. 1875, Prince Napoléon, Rec. 155, concl. David (France).

United States—Restrictions on Imports of Cotton and Man-Made Fibre Underwear (*United States—Underwear*) (1997) WTO/DS24/AB/R (Appellate Body Report) online: World Trade Organization http://www.wto.org/english/tratop_e/dispu_e/ab_reports_e.htm.

United States—Measures Relating to Shrimp from Thailand (2008) WT/DS343/R (Appellate Body Report) online: World Trade Organization http://www.wto.org/english/tratop_e/dispu_e/ab_reports_e.htm.

Treaties

Statute of the International Court of Justice, online: international Court of Justice http://www.icj-cij.org/documents/index.php?p1=4&p2=2&p3=0.

General Agreement on Tariffs and Trade, 30 October 1947, 58 NTS 187, Can TS 1947 No. 27.

Treaty Establishing the European Community (*Nice consolidated version*), 24 December 2002, Official Journal C 325, 24/12/2002 P. 0135–0135, online: European Union http://eur-lex.europa.eu/LexUriServ/LexUriServ.do?uri=CELEX:12002E253:EN:HTML.

Charter of Fundamental Rights of the European Union, 18 December 2000, (2000/C 364/01) online: European Union http://www.europarl.europa.eu/charter/default_en.htm.

Vienna Convention on the Law of Treaties, 23 May 1969, UNTS 18232.

Regulatory and Policy Materials

Basel Committee on Banking Supervision. "Basel Committee Broadens Its Membership" (2009) online: Bank for International Settlements http://www.bis.org/press/p090610.htm.

Basel Committee on Banking Supervision. "Basel Committee Cooperation with Other Standard-setting Bodies" (Accessed on 20 April 2016) online: Bank for International Settlements www.bis.org/bcbs/coop_with_sec_and_ins.htm.

Basel Committee on Banking Supervision. "Basel Committee Membership" (Accessed on 25 April 2016) online: Bank for International Settlements http://www.bis.org/bcbs/membership.htm.

Basel Committee on Banking Supervision. "Basel Committee on Banking Supervision" (Accessed on 25 April 2016) online: Bank for International Settlements http://www.bis.org/bcbs/index.htm.

Basel Committee on Banking Supervision. "Basel III Liquidity Standard and Strategy for Assessing Implementation of Standards Endorsed by Group of Governors and Heads of Supervision" (8 January 2012) online: Bank for International Settlements http://www.bis.org/press/p120108.htm.

Basel Committee on Banking Supervision. "Basel III: A Global Regulatory Framework for more Resilient Banks and Banking Systems" (December 2010) online: Bank for International Settlements https://www.bis.org/publ/bcbs189_dec2010.htm.

Basel Committee on Banking Supervision. "Basel III: International Framework for Liquidity Risk Measurement, Standards and Monitoring" (December 2010) online: Bank for International Settlements https://www.bis.org/publ/bcbs188.htm.

Basel Committee on Banking Supervision. "Capital Requirements for Bank Exposures to Central Counterparties" (2012) online: Bank for International Settlements http://www.bis.org/publ/bcbs227.htm.

Basel Committee on Banking Supervision. "Core Principles for Effective Banking Supervision" (September 1997) online: Bank for International Settlements http://www.bis.org/publ/bcbs30a.htm.

Basel Committee on Banking Supervision. "Core Principles for Effective Banking Supervision" (2012) online: Bank for International Settlements http://www.bis.org/publ/bcbs230.htm.

Basel Committee on Banking Supervision. "Expansion of Membership Announced by the Basel Committee" (13 March 2009) online: Bank for International Settlements http://www.bis.org/press/p090313.htm.

Basel Committee on Banking Supervision. "Financial Market Developments and the Work of the Basel Committee" (9 October 2007) online: Bank for International Settlements http://www.bis.org/press/p071009.htm.

Basel Committee on Banking Supervision. "G10 Central Bank Governors and Heads of Supervision Endorse the Publication of the Revised Capital Framework" (26 June 2004) online: Bank for International Settlements http://www.bis.org/press/p040626.htm.

Basel Committee on Banking Supervision. "Good Practice Principles on Supervisory Colleges—Final Document" (2010) online: Bank for International Settlements http://www.bis.org/publ/bcbs177.htm.

Basel Committee on Banking Supervision. "Group of Governors and Heads of Supervision Announces Higher Global Minimum Capital Standards" (September 2010) online: Bank for International Settlements http://www.bis.org/press/p100912.htm.

Basel Committee on Banking Supervision. "Group of Governors and Heads of Supervision Endorses Revised Liquidity Standard for Banks" (2013) online: Bank for International Settlements http://www.bis.org/press/p130106.htm.

Basel Committee on Banking Supervision. "Group of Governors and Heads of Supervision Endorses Revised Liquidity Standard for Banks" (6 January 2013) online: Bank for International Settlements http://www.bis.org/press/p130106.pdf.

Basel Committee on Banking Supervision. "Guidance for National Authorities Operating the Countercyclical Capital Buffer" (December 2010) online: Bank for International Settlements http://www.bis.org/publ/bcbs187.htm.

Basel Committee on Banking Supervision. "History" (Accessed on 25 April 2016) online: Bank for International Settlements http://www.bis.org/bcbs/history.htm.

Basel Committee on Banking Supervision. "Initiatives on Capital Announced by the Basel Committee" (12 March 2009) online: Bank for International Settlements http://www.bis.org/press/p090312.htm.

Basel Committee on Banking Supervision. "International Convergence of Capital Measurement and Capital Standards" (1988) online: Bank for International Settlements http://www.bis.org/publ/bcbs04a.htm.

Basel Committee on Banking Supervision. "International Regulatory Framework for Banks (Basel III)" (Accessed on 25 April 2016) online: Bank for International Settlements http://www.bis.org/bcbs/basel3.htm.

Basel Committee on Banking Supervision. "Liquidity Coverage Ratio Disclosure Standards—Consultative Document" (2013) online: Bank for International Settlements http://www.bis.org/publ/bcbs259.htm.

Basel Committee on Banking Supervision. "Main Expert Sub-Committees" (Accessed on 25 April 2016) online: Bank for International Settlements http://www.bis.org/bcbs/mesc.htm.

Basel Committee on Banking Supervision. "Monitoring Adoption of Basel III Standards and Reports to the G20" (Accessed on 25 April 2016) online: Bank for International Settlements http://www.bis.org/bcbs/implementation/bprl1.htm.

Basel Committee on Banking Supervision. "Operational Risk—Supervisory Guidelines for the Advanced Measurement Approaches—Final Document" (2011) online: Bank for International Settlements http://www.bis.org/publ/bcbs196.htm.

Basel Committee on Banking Supervision. "Outcome of the Consultative Process on Proposals for International Convergence of Capital Measurement and Capital Standards" (July 1988) online: Bank for International Settlements http://www.bis.org/publ/bcbs04b.pdf.

Basel Committee on Banking Supervision. "Principles for Enhancing Corporate Governance—Final Document" (2010) online: Bank for International Settlements http://www.bis.org/publ/bcbs176.htm.

Basel Committee on Banking Supervision. "Principles for Sound Liquidity Risk Management and Supervision" (17 June 2008) online: Bank for International Settlements http://www.bis.org/press/p080617.htm.

Basel Committee on Banking Supervision. "Proposals for International Convergence of Capital Measurement and Standards—Consultative Document" (December 1987) online: Bank for International Settlements http://www.bis.org/publ/bcbs03a.htm.

Basel Committee on Banking Supervision. "Proposed Revisions to the Basel II Market Risk Framework" (July 2008) online: Bank for International Settlements http://www.bis.org/publ/bcbs140.htm.

Basel Committee on Banking Supervision, "Reducing Variation In Credit Risk-Weighted Assets—Constraints on the use of Internal Model Approaches—Consultative Document" (March 2016) online: Bank for International Settlements https://www.bis.org/bcbs/publ/d362.htm.

Basel Committee on Banking Supervision, "Regulatory Consistency Assessment Programme (RCAP)—Analysis of Risk-Weighted Assets for Credit Risk in the Banking Book" (April 2016) online: Bank for International Settlements https://www.bis.org/bcbs/publ/d363.htm.

Basel Committee on Banking Supervision. "Report and Recommendations of the Cross-border Bank Resolution Group—Final Paper" (March 2010) online: Bank for International Settlements http://www.bis.org/publ/bcbs169.htm.

Basel Committee on Banking Supervision. "Report on the Supervision of Banks' Foreign Establishments—Concordat" (September 1975) online: Bank for International Settlements http://www.bis.org/publ/bcbs00a.htm.

Basel Committee on Banking Supervision. "Revisions to the Basel III Leverage Ratio Framework—Consultative Document" (April 2016) online: Bank for International Settlements https://www.bis.org/bcbs/publ/d365.htm.

BCBS, "Report to G20 Leaders on Monitoring Implementation of Basel III Regulatory Reforms (August 2013) online: BIS http://www.bis.org/publ/bcbs260.pdf.

Basel Committee on Banking Supervision. "Sound Practices for Backtesting Counterparty Credit Risk Models—Final Document" (2010) online: Bank for International Settlements http://www.bis.org/publ/bcbs185.htm.

Basel Committee on Banking Supervision. "Supervisory Guidance for Managing Risks Associated with the Settlement of Foreign Exchange Transactions" (2013) online: Bank for International Settlements http://www.bis.org/publ/bcbs241.htm.

Basel Committee on Banking Supervision. "The Basel Committee's Work" (Accessed on 22 April 2016) online: Bank for International Settlements http://www.bis.org/bcbs/bcbs_work.htm.

Basel Committee on Banking Supervision. *Basel Committee on Banking Supervision (BCBS) Charter* (January 2013) online: Bank for International Settlements http://www.bis.org/bcbs/charter.htm.

Financial Crisis Inquiry Commission. "Final Report of the National Commission on the Causes of the Financial and Economic Crisis in the United States" (2011) online: Financial Crisis Inquiry Commission http://FCIC-static.law.stanford.edu/cdn_media/FCIC-reports/FCIC_final_report_full.pdf.

Financial Services Authority. "Turner Review: A Regulatory Response to the Global Banking Crisis" (2009) online: Financial Services Authority http://www.fsa.gov.uk/pubs/other/turner_review.pdf.

Financial Stability Board. "Addressing Financial System Procyclicality: A Possible Framework" (April 2009) online: Financial Stability Board http://www.financialstabilityboard.org/publications/r_0904e.htm.

Financial Stability Board. "Compendium of Standards" (Accessed on 25 April 2016) online: Financial Stability Board http://www.financialstabilityboard.org/cos/index.htm.

Financial Stability Board. "FSB Plenary, Committees and Regional Consultative Groups (RCGS) Membership" (Accessed on 25 April 2016) online: Financial Stability Board http://www.fsb.org/about/pac/.

Financial Stability Board. "Implementing OTC Derivatives Market Reforms" (October 2010) online: Financial Stability Board http://www.financialstabilityboard.org/list/fsb_pa/tid_172/index.htm.

Financial Stability Board. "Key Standards for Sound Financial Systems" (Accessed on 25 April 2016) online: Financial Stability Board http://www.financialstabilityboard.org/cos/key_standards.htm.

Financial Stability Board. "Macroprudential Policy Tools and Frameworks—Update to G20 Finance Ministers and Central Bank Governors" (February 2011) online: Financial Stability Board http://www.financialstabilityboard.org/list/fsb_pa/tid_161/index.htm.

Financial Stability Board. "Monitoring Note on the Effects of Regulatory Reforms on Emerging Market and Developing Economies" (12 September 2013) online: Bank for International Settlements https://www.financialstabilityboard.org/publications/r_130912.htm.

Financial Stability Board. "Policy Measures to Address Systemically Important Financial Institutions" (November 2011) online: Financial Stability Board http://www.financialstabilityboard.org/publications/r_111104bb.pdf.

Financial Stability Board. "To G20 Finance Ministers and Central Bank Governors Financial Reforms—Progress and Challenges" (17 February 2014) online: G20 Library https://www.g20.org/official_resources/library.

Financial Stability Forum. "Report of the Financial Stability Forum on Enhancing Market and Institutional Resilience" (April 2008) online: Financial Stability Board http://www.financialstabilityboard.org/publications/r_0804.pdf.

Foreign & Commonwealth Office. "Treaties and MOUs: Guidance on Practice and Procedures" (March 2013) online: Government Digital Service: https://www.gov.uk/government/publications/treaties-and-mous-guidance-on-practice-and-procedures.

FSB. "Compendium of Standards" (Accessed on 25 April 2016) online: FSB http://www.fsb.org/what-we-do/about-the-compendium-of-standards/.

G20. "2008 Washington" (Accessed on 21 June 2015) online: G20 https://www.g20.org/about_g20/past_summits/2008_washington.

G20. "Declaration of the Summit on Financial Markets and the World Economy Washington Summit" (15 November 2008) online: G20 Information Centre www.g20.utoronto.ca/2008/2008declaration1115.html.

G20. "Declaration on Strengthening the Financial System" (April 2009) online: G20 Information Centrehttp://www.g20.utoronto.ca/2009/2009ifi.pdf.

G20. "Declaration-Summit on Financial Markets and the World Economy" (15 November 2008) online: G20 https://www.g20.org/sites/default/files/g20_resources/library/Washington_Declaration_0.pdf.

G20. "Final Communiqué: Meeting of G20 Finance Ministers and Central Bank Governors" (20 April 2012) online: G20 Information Centre http://www.g20.utoronto.ca/2012/2012-120420-finance-en.html.

G20. "G20 Leaders Deceleration" (Las Cabos, Mexico, 19 June 2012) online: G20 Information Centre http://www.g20.utoronto.ca/2012/2012-0619-loscabos.html.

G20. "Global Plan Annex: Declaration on Strengthening the Financial System" (Statement Issued by the G20 Leaders London, 2 April 2009) online: G20 Information Centre http://www.g20.utoronto.ca/2009/2009ifi.html.

G20. "Global Plan for Recovery and Reform" (Statement Issued by the G20 Leaders London, 2 April 2009) online: G20 Research Group http://www.g20.utoronto.ca/2009/2009communique0402.html.

G7. "Declaration of G7 Finance Ministers and Central Bank Governors" (30 October 1998) online: International Monetary Fund http://www.imf.org/external/np/g7/103098dc.htm.

Global Partnership for Financial Inclusion. "About the G20" online: Global Partnership for Financial Inclusion http://gpfi.org/about-gpfi/about-the-g20.

Group of Banking Supervisors from Central and Eastern Europe. "Contact Information of International Groups of Supervisors" (Accessed on 25 April 2016) online: http://www.bscee.org/groups/groups.html.

Independent Evaluation Group. "About IEG: Improving World Bank Group Development Results Through Excellence in Evaluation" (2013) online: Independent Evaluation Group http://ieg.worldbankgroup.org/about-us.

Independent Evaluation Office. "Report on the Evaluation of the Financial Sector Assessment Program" (5 January 2006) online: Independent Evaluation Office http://www.ieo-imf.org/eval/complete/eval_01052006.html.

Inspection Panel. "About Us" (2013) online: World Bank: http://web.worldbank.org/WBSITE/EXTERNAL/EXTINSPECTIONPANEL/0,,menuPK:64129249~pagePK:64132081~piPK:64132052~theSitePK:380794,00.html.

Inspection Panel. "Panel Resolution and Mandate" (2013) online: World Bank http://web.worldbank.org/WBSITE/EXTERNAL/EXTINSPECTIONPANEL/0,, contentMDK:20173262~menuPK:64129254~pagePK:64129751~piPK:64128378~theSitePK:380794,00.html.

International Monetary Fund. "Financial Sector Assessment Program (FSAP)" (12 February 2014) online: International Monetary Fund https://www.imf.org/external/np/fsap/fssa.aspx.

International Monetary Fund. "Financial Sector Assessment: A Handbook" (29 September 2005) online: International Monetary Fund http://www.imf.org/external/pubs/ft/fsa/eng/.

International Monetary Fund. "Global Financial Stability Report" (April 2006) online: International Monetary Fund. http://www.imf.org/External/Pubs/FT/GFSR/2006/01/pdf/chp2.pdf.

Office of the Ombudsperson. "An Independent and Impartial Ombudsperson, Who Reviews Requests From Individuals, Groups, undertakings or Entities Seeking to be Removed from the Al-Qaida Sanctions List of the Security Council's Al-Qaida Sanctions Committee" (2013) online: United Nations http://www.un.org/en/sc/ombudsperson/.

Security Council Committee Pursuant to Resolutions 1267 (1999) and 1989 (2011) Concerning Al-Qaida and Associated Individuals and Entities, "Guidelines of the Committee for the Conduct of Its Work" (2013) online: United Nations http://www.un.org/sc/committees/1267/pdf/1267_guidelines.pdf.

United Nations Security Council. "Focal Point for De-listing Established Pursuant to Security Council Resolution 1730" (2006) online: United Nations http://www.un.org/sc/committees/dfp.shtml.

United Nations Security Council. "Security Council Sanctions Committees: An Overview" (Accessed on 25 April 2016) online: United Nations http://www.un.org/sc/committees/.

United Nations. "Monterrey Consensus of the International Conference on Financing for Development" (International Conference on Financing for Development, 2002) online: UN http://www.un.org/esa/ffd/monterrey/MonterreyConsensus.pdf.

United Nations. "The Security Council" (Accessed on 25 April 2016) online: United Nations http://www.un.org/en/sc/.

United States Department of State. "Circular 175 Procedure" (Accessed on 25 April 2016) online: Bureau of Public Affairs http://www.state.gov/s/l/treaty/c175/.

United States Department of Treasury. "The Financial Crisis Response in Charts" (2012) online: United States Department of Treasury http://www.treasury.gov/resource-center/data-chart- center/Documents/20120413_FinancialCrisisResponse.pdf.

World Bank. "Financial Inclusion Data" (Accessed on 25 April 2016) online: World Bank http://datatopics.worldbank.org/financialinclusion/.

World Trade Organization. "Legal Texts: the WTO agreements" (2013) online: World Trade Organization http://www.wto.org/english/docs_e/legal_e/ursum_e.htm#General.

World Trade Organization. "Procedures for the Circulation and De-restriction of WTO Documents" (2002) T/L/452, online: World Trade Organization http://members.wto.org/WTO_resources/documentation/derestriction_e.htm.

World Trade Organization. "Reports of the Subsidiary Bodies to the General Council for Trade in Goods" (1996) online: World Trade Organization http://www.wto.org/english/thewto_e/minist_e/min96_e/w46-2.pdf.

World Trade Organization. "The Process—Stages in a Typical WTO Dispute Settlement Case" online: World Trade Organization http://www.wto.org/english/tratop_e/dispu_e/disp_settlement_cbt_e/c6s2p1_e.htm.

Books and Book Chapters

Aronson, Mark I., Bruce Douglas Dyer & Matthew Groves. *Judicial Review of Administrative Action*, 3rd ed (Pyrmont, NSW: Lawbook Co, 2004).

Barker, Rdoney. "Democratic Legitimation: What Is It, Who Wants It, and Why?" in Achim Hurrelmann, Steffen Schneider & Jens Steffek, ed. *Legitimacy In an Age of Global Politics* (New York: Palgrave Macmillan, 2007) 19.

Barth, James R., Gerard Caprio Jr. & Ross Levine, *Guardians of Finance: Making Regulators Work for Us* (Cambridge, MA: MIT Press, 2012).

Blunden, George. "Control and Supervision of the Foreign Operations of Banks" in John Edvin Wadsworth et al., eds, *The Development of Financial Institutions in Europe 1956–1976* (Leyden: Sijthoff, 1977).

Bradlow, Daniel D. & Andria N. Fourie. "Independent Accountability Mechanisms at International and Regional Development Banks" in Thomase Hale & David Held, eds, *Handbook of Innovations in Transnational Governance* (Cambridge: Polity Press, 2011) 122.

Bradlow, Daniel D. & Andria N. Fourie. "Independent Accountability Mechanisms at International and Regional Development Banks" in Thomase Hale & David Held, eds, *Handbook of Innovations in Transnational Governance* (Cambridge: Polity Press, 2011) 122.

Brummer, Chris. *Soft Law and the Global Financial System: Rule Making in the 21st Century* (Cambridge; New York: Cambridge University Press, 2012).

Camilli, Enrico L. "Basel–Brussels One Way? The EU in the Legalization Process of Basel Soft Law" in Edoardo Chiti & Bernardo G. Mattarella, eds, *Global Administrative Law and EU Administrative Law: Relationships, Legal Issues and Comparison* (Berlin: Springer, 2011) 324.

Cohen, Joshua. "Deliberation and Democratic Legitimacy" in James Bohman & William Rehg, *Deliberative Democracy: Essays on Reason and Politics* (MIT Press, 1997) 67.

Craig, Paul P. *EU Administrative Law* (New York: Oxford University Press, 2006).

Dahl, Robert A. "Can International Organizations Be Democratic? A Skeptic's View" in Ian Shapiro & Casiano Hacker-Cordón, eds. Democracy's edges (New York: Cambridge University Press, 1999).

Davies, Howard & David Green. *Global Financial Regulation—The Essential Guide* (Cambridge: Polity, 2008).

Davis, Howard. *The Financial Crisis: Who is to Blame* (Cambridge: Polity Press, 2010).

Dewatripont Mathias et al., *Balancing the Banks: Global Lessons from the Financial Crisis* (Princeton: Princeton University Press, 2010).

Dworkin, Ronald. *Law's Empire* (Cambridge, MA: Belknap Press of Harvard University Press, 1986).

Feinaugle, Clemens A. "The UN Security Council Al-Qaida and Taliban Sanctions Committee: Emerging Principles of International Institutional Law for the Protection of Individuals?" in Bogdandy et al., eds, *The Exercise of Public Authority by International Institutions: Advancing International Institutional Law* (New York: Springer, 2010) 101.

Florini, Ann. "The Battle over Transparency" in Ann Florini, ed, *The Right to Know: Transparency for an Open World* (New York: Columbia University Press, 2007) 1.

Franck, Thomas M. *The power of legitimacy among nations* (New York : Oxford University Press, 1990).

French, Kenneth R. et al., *The Squam Lake Report: Fixing the Financial System* (Princeton: Princeton University Press, 2010).

Fuller, Lon L. *The Morality of Law* (New Haven: Yale University Press, 1964).

Gall, Gerald L. *The Canadian legal system*, 5th ed (Ont.: Carswell, 2004).

Giacinto della Cananea. "The Giving Reasons Requirement: A Global Standard for Public Authorities" in Giacinto Della Cananea & Aldo Sandulli, *Global Standards for Public Authorities* (Editoriale Scientifica, 2012).

Giovanoli, Mario. "A New Architecture for the Global Financial Market: Legal Aspects of International Financial Standard Setting" in Mario Giovanoli, ed, *International Monetary Law, Issues for the New Millennium* (Oxford: Oxford University Press, 2000) 3.

Goode, Roy. *Commercial Law*, 2d ed (London: Penguin, 1995).

Goodhart, Charles A. E. *The Basel Committee on Banking Supervision: A History of the Early Years, 1974–1997* (Cambridge, UK; New York: Cambridge University Press, 2011).

Goodhart, Charles E. et al., *Financial Regulation: Why, How and Where Now* (London: Routledge, 1998).

Goodhart, Charles E. "How Should We Regulate the Financial Sector" in Adair Turner et al., *The Future of Finance and the Theory that Underpins It* (London School of Economics, 2010) 165.

Greenspan, Alan. "The Crisis" in David Homer & Justin Wolfers, eds, *Brookings Papers on Economic Activity* (Brookings Instituion Press, 2010) 201.

Greenspan, Alan. *The Age of Turbulence: Adventures in a New World* (New York: Penguin Press, 2007).

Held, David. *Democracy and the Global Order: Form the Modern States to Cosmopolitan Governance* (Polity Press: Cambridge, 1995).

Hurrelmann, Achim, Steffen Schneider & Jens Steffek. "Introduction: Legitimacy in an Age of Global Politics" in Achim Hurrelmann, Steffen Schneider & Jens Steffek, eds, *Legitimacy In an Age of Global Politics* (New York: Palgrave Macmillan, 2007).

James, Harold. *Making the European Monetary Union* (United States: Bank for International Settlement, 2012).

Jarsulic, Marc. *Anatomy of a Financial Crisis: A Real Estate Bubble, Runaway Credit Markets, and Regulatory Failure* (New York: Palgrave, 2010).

Johnston, Robert B. *The Economics of the Euro-Market: History, Theory and Policy* (London: McMillan Press, 1983).

Kenen, Peter B. *The International Financial Architecture: What's New? What's Missing?* (Washington: Institute for International Economics, 2001).

Peter, Fabienne. *Democratic legitimacy* (New York: Routledge, 2009).

Porter, Tony. *States, Markets, and Regimes in Global Finance* (New York: St. Martin's Press, 1993).

Sarra, Janis P. "Embedding Fairness as a Fundamental Norm in Financial Markets", in Janis Sarra, ed, *An Exploration of Fairness: Interdisciplinary Inquiries in Law, Science and the Humanities* (Carswell: Canada, 2013) 194.

Scharpf, Fritz W. *Governing In Europe: Effective and Democratic?* (Oxford: Oxford University Press, 1999).

Scholte, Jan A. "Global Governance, Accountability, and Civil Society" in Jan A. Scholte, ed, *Building Global Democracy: Civil Society and Accountable Global Governance* (New York: Cambridge University Press, 2011).

Schuler, Gefion. "Effective Governance through Decentralized Soft Implementation: The OECD Guidelines for Multinational Enterprises" in Armin V. Bogdandy et al., eds, *The Exercise of Public Authority by International Institutions: Advancing International Institutional Law* (New York: Springer, 2010) 197.

Seerden René & Frits Stroink, eds. *Administrative Law of the European Union, Its Member States and the United States: A Comparative Analysis* (Cambridge, UK: Intersentia, 2002).

Shapiro, Martin. "The Institutionalization of European Administrative Space" in Alec S. Sweet, Wayne Sandholtz & Neil Fligstein, eds, *The Institutionalisation of Europe* (New York: Oxford University Press, 2001) 94.

Simon Gleeson, *International Regulation of Banking—Basel II: Capital and Risk Requirements* (Oxford, New York: Oxford University Press, 2010).

Slaughter, Anne-Marie. *A New World Order* (Princeton, NJ: Princeton University Press, 2004).

Stiglitz, Joseph et al., *The Stiglitz Report: Reforming the International Monetary and Financial Systems in the Wake of the Global Crisis* (New York: The New Press, 2010).

Tarullo, Daniel K. *Banking on Basel: Future of Financial Regulation* (Washington: PetersonInstitute for International Economics, 2008).

Taylor, John B. *Getting Off Track: How Government Actions and Interventions Caused, Prolonged, and Worsened the Financial Crisis* (California: Hoover Institution Press, 2009).

Turan, Ilter. "Democracy, Types of" in Bertrand Badie, Dirk Berg-Schlosser & Leonardo Morlino, eds, *International Encyclopaedia of Political Science* (Thousand Oaks, CA: Sage Publications, 2011).

Vestergard, Jakob. *Discipline in Global Economy: International Finance and End of Liberalism* (New York: Routledge, 2009).

Wade, William & Christopher Forsyth. *Administrative Law*, 10th ed (New York: Oxford University Press, 2009).

Walker, George A. *International Banking Regulation: Law, Policy, and Practice* (London, UK: Kluwer, 2001).

Weber, Max. *Economy and Society: An Outline of Interpretive Society* (Berkley: University of Californian Press, 1978).

Wet, Erika D. "Holding International Institutions Accountable: The Complementary Role of Non-Judicial Oversight Mechanisms and Judicial Review" in Armin V. Bogdandy et al., eds, *The Exercise of Public Authority by International Institutions: Advancing International Institutional Law* (New York: Springer, 2010) 855.

Windsor, Joseph. "The WTO Committee on Trade in Financial Services: The Exercise of Public Authority within an Informational Forum" in V. Bogdandy et al., eds, *The Exercise of Public Authority by International Institutions: Advancing International Institutional Law* (New York: Springer, 2010) 405.

Articles

"A World Banking Crisis", *The Economist* 6832 (3 August 1974) 55.

"Financial Crisis: Gordon Brown Calls for 'New Bretton Woods'" *The Telegraph* (13 October 2008) online: The Telegraph www.telegraph.co.uk.

"Global Recession Timeline", *BBC News* (Accessed on 25 April 2016) online: BBC http://news.bbc.co.uk/2/hi/business/8242825.stm.

Acharya, Viral V. & Matthew P. Richardson. "Causes of the Financial Crisis" (2009) 21:2–3 *Critical Review* 195.

Admati et al., Anat R. "Healthy Banking System Is the Goal, Not the Profitable Banks", *Financial Times* (9 November 2010).

Admati et al., Anat R. "Fallacies, Irrelevant Facts, and Myths in the Discussion of Capital Regulation: Why Bank Equity is Not Socially Expensive" (2011) online: SSRN http://papers.ssrn.com/sol3/papers.cfm?abstract_id=1669704.

Ala'i, Padideh. "From the Periphery to the Center? The Evolving WTO Jurisprudence on Transparency and Good Governance" (2008) 11:4 J Int'l Econ L 779.

Allaire, Yvan & Mihaela E. Firsirotu. "The Fall of Wall Street: How the Crisis Was Made and How It Could Have Been Avoided" (April 2009) online: SSRN http://ssrn.com/abstract=1514902.

Arner, Douglas W. "The Global Credit Crisis of 2008: Causes and Consequences" (AIIFL Working Paper No. 3, 2009) online: SSRN http://papers.ssrn.com/sol3/papers.cfm?abstract_id=1330744.

Atik, Jeffery. "Basel II: A Post-Crisis Post-Mortem" (2011) 19 Transnat'l L & Contemp Probs 731.

Barr, Michael S. & Geoffrey P. Miller. "Global Administrative Law: The View from Basel" (2006) 17:1 EJIL 15.

Bernanke, Ben. "Modern Risk Management and Banking Supervision" (12 June 2006) online: Federal Reserve http://www.federalreserve.gov/newsevents/speech/Bernanke20060612a.htm.

Brimmer, Andrew F. & Fredrick R. Dahl. "Growth of American International Banking: Implications for Public Policy" (1975) 30:2 *Journal of Finance* 341.

Buchanan, Allen & Robert O. Keohane. "The Legitimacy of Global Governance Institutions" (2006) 20:4 *Ethics and International Affairs* 405.

Case, Karl E. & Robert Shiller. "Is There a Bubble in the Housing Market?" (Brookings Paper on Economic Activity, No. 2, 2003) online: Brookings Institution http://www.brookings.edu/~/media/Files/Programs/ES/BPEA/2003_2_bpea_papers/2003b_bpea_caseshiller.pdf.

Coleman, William D. & Tony Porter. "International Institutions, Globalisation and Democracy: Assessing the Challenges" (2000) 14:3 *Global Society* 377.

Dam, Kenneth W. "The Subprime Crisis and Financial Regulation: International and Comparative Perspectives" (2010) 10 Chi J Int'l L 581.

Demirjuc-Kunt, Asli. "Measuring Financial Exclusion: How Many People Are Unbanked?" (24 April 2014) online: Consultative Group to Assist the Poor http://www.cgap.org/blog/measuring-financial-exclusion-how-many-people-are-unbanked.

Esty, Daniel C. "Good Governance at the Supranational Scale: Globalizing Administrative Law" (2006) 115 *Yale Law Journal* 1490.

Friedman, Hershey H. & Linda W. Friedman. "The Global Financial Crisis of 2008: What Went Wrong?" (9 March 2009) online: SSRN: http://dx.doi.org/10.2139/ssrn.1356193.

Giovanoli, Mario. "The Reform of the International Financial Architecture after the Global Crisis" (2009) 42 *International Law and Politics* 81.

Gutherie, Peter. "Security Council Sanctions and the Protection of Individual Rights" (2004) 60 NYU ANN SURV AM L 491.

Harlow, Carol. "Global Administrative Law: The Quest for Principles and Values" (2006) 17:1 EJIL 182.

Helleiner, Eric & Stefano Pagliari. "Towards a New Bretton Woods? The First G20 Leaders Summit and the Regulation of Global Finance" (2009) 14:2 *New Political Economy* 276.

Hellwig, Martin. "Capital Regulation after the Crisis: Business as Usual?" (Max Planck Institute for Research on Collective Goods, July 2010) online: Max Plank Institute http://www.coll.mpg.de/pdf_dat/2010_31online.pdf.

Herring, Richard J. "The Known, the Unknown, and the Unknowable in Financial Policy: An Application to the Subprime Crisis" (2009) 26 Yale J on Reg 391.

Hey, Ellen. "The World Bank Inspection Panel: Towards the Recognition of a New Legally Relevant Relationship in International Law" (1997) 2 Hofstra L & Pol'y Symp 61.

Horta, Korinna. "Rhetoric and Reality: Human Rights and the World Bank" (2002) 15 Harv Hum Rts J 227.

Independent Evaluation Group. "About IEG: Improving World Bank Group Development Results through Excellence in Evaluation" (2013) online: Independent Evaluation Group http://ieg.worldbankgroup.org/about-us.

Kapstein, Ethan B. "Architects of Stability? International Cooperation among Financial Supervisors" (Paper prepared for the Bank for International Settlements 75th Anniversary Conference Basel, Switzerland, June 2005).

Keohane, Robert O. "Global Governance and Legitimacy" (2011) 18:1 *Review of International Political Economy* 99.

Kingsbury, Benedict, Nico Krisch & Richard B Stewart. "The Emergence of Global Administrative Law" (2005) 68:15 Law & Contemp Probs 15.

Kingsbury, Benedict. "The Administrative Law Frontier in Global Governance" (2005) 99 Am Soc'y Int'l L Proc 143.

Kling, Arnold. "Not What They Had in Mind: A History of Policies that Produced the Financial Crisis of 2008" (2009) online: SSRN http://ssrn.com/abstract=3D1474430.

Laeven, Luc & Fabian Valencia. "Resolution of Banking Crises: The Good, the Bad, and the Ugly" (IMF Working Paper, WP/10/146, June 2010).

Manin, Bernard. "On Legitimacy and Political Deliberation" (1987) 15:3 *Political Theory* 338.

Marceau Gabrielle & Mikella Hurley. "Transparency and Public Participation in the WTO: A Report Card on WTO Transparency Mechanisms" (2012) 4:1 TRADE L & DEV 19.

Meyer, Perry. Book Review of *Morality of Law* by Lon L. Fuller, (1964) 10 McGill L J 380.

Noonan, Laura, "Basel IV Spectre Looms For Battle-Worn Bankers" *The Financial Times* (14 March 2016).

Norton, Joseph J. "The Work of the Basle Supervisors Committee on Bank Capital Adequacy and the July 1988 Report on 'International Convergence of Capital Measurement and Capital Standards'" (1989) 23 Int'l Law 245.

Parker, George & Daniel Dombey. "European Call for 'Bretton Woods II' ", *The Financial Times* (16 October 2008) online: Financial Times http://www.ft.com.

Pauwelyn, Joost, Ramses A. Wessel & Jan Wouters. "The Exercise of Public Authority through Informal International Lawmaking: An Accountability Issue?" (Jean Monnet Working Paper 06/11, New York University School of Law, 2011).

Peihani, Maziar. "The Global Financial Crisis of 2008: An Analysis of Contributing Trends, Policies and Failures" (2012) 27:3 BFLR 465.

Prakash, Anupam. "Evolution of the Basel Framework on Bank Capital Regulation" (Reserve Bank of India Occasional Papers Vol. 29, No. 2, Monsoon, 2008).

Roos, Stephanie R. "The World Bank Inspection Panel in Its Seventh Year: An Analysis of Its Process, Mandate, and Desirability with Special Reference to the China (Tibet) Case" (2001) 5 *Max Planck Yearbook of United Nations Law* 473.

Scholte, Jan A. Towards Greater Legitimacy in Global Governance (2011) 18:1 *Review of International Political Economy* 110.

Slaughter, Anne-Marie. "Agencies on the Loose? Holding Government Networks Accountable" (Public Law and Legal Theory Working Paper No. 006, 1999) online: SSRN http://papers.ssrn.com/sol3/papers.cfm?abstract_id=209319.

Slaughter, Anne-Marrie & Zaring, David. "Networks Go International: An Update" (2006) 6:12 *Annual Review of Law and Social Science* 215.

Steffek, Jens. "Legitimation of International Governance: A Discourse Approach" (2003) 9 *European Journal of International Relations* 249.

Verick, Sher & Iyanatul Islam. "The Great Recession of 2008–2009: Causes, Consequences and Policy Responses" (IZA Discussion Paper No. 4934, 2009) online: SSRN http://papers.ssrn.com/sol3/papers.cfm?abstract_id=1631069.

Zaring, David. "Informal Procedure, Hard and Soft, in International Administration" (2005) 5: 2 Chi J Int'l L 547.

Speeches and Testimonies

Bernanke, Ben. "The Economic Outlook" (Testimony before the Joint Economic Committee, U.S. Congress, 28 March 2007) online: Federal Reserve http://www.federalreserve.gov/newsevents/testimony/bernanke20070328a.htm.

Cox, Christopher. Address (Speech delivered at the Security Traders 12th Annual Washington Conference, 7 May 2008) online: United States Securities and Exchange Commission http://www.sec.gov/news/speech/2008/spch050708cc.htm.

Cox, Christopher. "The State of the United States Economy and Financial Markets" (Testimony before the U.S. Senate Committee on Banking, Housing and Urban Affairs, 14 February 2008) online: United States Securities and Exchange Commission http://www.sec.gov/news/testimony/2008/ts021408cc.htm.

Geithner, Timothy F. (Written Testimony House Financial Services Committee Hearing, 24 march 2009) online: United States Department of Treasury http://www.treasury.gov/press-center/press-releases/Pages/tg67.aspx.

Geithner, Timothy F. (Written Testimony before the House Committee on Oversight and Government Reform, 27 January 2010) online: United States Department of Treasury http://www.treasury.gov/press-center/press-releases/Pages/tg514.aspx.

Geithner, Timothy F. "Reducing Systemic Risk in a Dynamic Financial System" (Remarks at the Economic Club of New York, New York City, 9 June 2008) online: Federal Reserve Bank of New York http://www.newyorkfed.org/newsevents/speeches/2008/tfg080609.html.

Geithner, Timothy F. Address (Remarks before the American Enterprise Institute on Financial Reform, 22 March 2010) online: United States Department of Treasury http://www.treasury.gov/press-center/press-releases/Pages/tg600.aspx.

www.ingramcontent.com/pod-product-compliance
Lightning Source LLC
Chambersburg PA
CBHW031331230926
51848CB00001B/190
* 9 7 8 9 0 0 4 3 2 8 1 2 9 *